THE QUEEN ART& IMAGE

THE QUEEN ART& IMAGE

PAUL MOORHOUSE
WITH AN ESSAY BY DAVID CANNADINE

NATIONAL PORTRAIT GALLERY, LONDON

GOD Save THE QUEEN

Sex PistOls

Published in Great Britain by
National Portrait Gallery Publications,
National Portrait Gallery, St Martin's Place,
London WC2H 0HE

Published on the occasion of the exhibition
The Queen: Art & Image at the
National Gallery Complex, Edinburgh,
from 25 June to 18 September 2011,
the Ulster Museum, Belfast, from
14 October 2011 to 15 January 2012,
the National Museum Cardiff,
from 4 February to 29 April 2012 and
the National Portrait Gallery, London,
from 17 May to 21 October 2012.

This exhibition has been made possible
with the assistance of the Government
Indemnity Scheme provided by the
Department for Culture, Media and Sport
and administered by the Museums,
Libraries and Archives Council.

For a complete catalogue
of current publications please write to
the address above, or visit our website at
www.npg.org.uk/publications

ISBN 978 1 85514 412 5 hardback
ISBN 978 1 85514 444 6 paperback

A catalogue record for this book is available
from the British Library.

10 9 8 7 6 5 4 3 2 1

Head of Publications: Celia Joicey
Managing Editor: Christopher Tinker
Editor: Claudia Bloch
Production Manager: Ruth Müller-Wirth
Design: Thomas Manss & Company
Printed in China

Front cover: Queen Elizabeth II by
Dorothy Wilding (hand-coloured by
Beatrice Johnson), 1952, page 59
Back cover: *Lightness of Being* by
Chris Levine, 2007, page 149

Edinburgh presentation
sponsored by Turcan Connell

FSC
www.fsc.org

MIX
Paper from
responsible sources
FSC® C003532

TURCAN CONNELL
SOLICITORS AND ASSET MANAGERS

CONTENTS

SPONSOR'S FOREWORD

As we approach this historic anniversary of Her Majesty's accession, Turcan Connell feels privileged to be involved in such a very special exhibition.

We are enthusiastic supporters of the arts and particularly value our long-standing relationship with the National Galleries of Scotland. It is great that we in Scotland are having the first opportunity to view this remarkable range of images.

For so many of us, there has been only one monarch and it is fascinating to see the way in which such different artists have portrayed the Queen over these six decades of Her Majesty's reign.

As a business, we have been regular sponsors of exhibitions, concerts and literary events, we have collected paintings and we have commissioned a wide range of works in diverse media. An artist in residence has worked with us over an extended period and we have hosted many cultural events in our offices. Our working days and our working lives have been enhanced and enlivened by this active engagement. We hope and believe that our staff and our clients have also experienced pleasure, interest and amusement from Turcan Connell's participation in the arts.

We thank all those who have contributed to the success of this exhibition.

DOUGLAS CONNELL
Joint Senior Partner, Turcan Connell
Turcan Connell is the sponsor of the Edinburgh presentation of *The Queen: Art & Image.*

FOREWORD

If Her Majesty is the most portrayed person in British history, this is not simply because of the length of her reign, but also because of the particular and huge esteem in which she is held. It is with great affection that she is personally admired, both as the United Kingdom's head of state and as the head of the royal family. The changing nature of regal portraiture offers a fascinating insight into a changing nation alongside a changing monarchy.

The National Portrait Gallery in London counts portraits of kings and queens as a special part of its Collection. The holdings span 500 years of British history from Henry VII, painted in the early sixteenth century, to the many photographic and painted portraits of the present Queen. Since its foundation in 1856, the Gallery has had a consistent ambition to secure important royal portraits. On occasions the celebration of royal portraiture has resulted in a new commission, on others by mounting an exhibition that extends beyond the Collection itself.

The Queen: Art & Image follows in a sequence of exhibitions, including *Elizabeth II: Portraits of Sixty Years* curated by Malcolm Rogers in 1986, but it differs in two important respects. Alongside outstanding studio portraits are more images of the Queen taken both on official and entirely informal occasions. Also selected are works by artists such as Gilbert and George, Gerhard Richter, Andy Warhol and Hew Locke that are not taken from life and offer an additional visual register.

The National Portrait Gallery is very pleased that the exhibition will be on display in four capital cities: Edinburgh, Belfast, Cardiff and London. I offer my thanks to fellow national directors and to the staff at all four institutions for contributing so much to the whole project.

I am delighted that KPMG is the sponsor of the London exhibition, and Turcan Connell for the showing in Edinburgh, with a range of further funders lending additional support across all of the exhibition tour venues. Their support has been crucial in making the whole enterprise possible.

I am most grateful to curator Paul Moorhouse, Curator of Twentieth-Century Portraits, who has written this book. I also wish to thank Professor Sir David Cannadine for his elegant and engaging essay, and Lord Janvrin; both have given advice and welcome support as Gallery Trustees. My thanks additionally go to a number of colleagues at the Royal Household and the Royal Collections Trust, for their invaluable help and support, including Christopher Geidt, Private Secretary to the Queen, Edward Young, Deputy Private Secretary to the Queen, and Doug King, Assistant Private Secretary to the Queen.

Finally, the National Portrait Gallery would like to thank Her Majesty The Queen, to whom this special tribute is dedicated for her Diamond Jubilee.

SANDY NAIRNE
Director, National Portrait Gallery, London

SIXTY YEARS
A QUEEN

SOME HISTORICAL REFLECTIONS
ON THE REIGN AND THE JUBILEES
OF ELIZABETH II

DAVID CANNADINE

On 7 February 1952, the Prime Minister, who was once again Winston Churchill, broadcast to the British nation, Empire and Commonwealth to pay a heartfelt tribute to King George VI, who had died the previous day. Now in peacetime, as he had so often done before in wartime, Churchill caught and crystallised the prevailing mood, paying eloquent homage to the late sovereign, who, along with his consort, had refused to leave the country in 1940 and had endured the Blitz with his people, and whose sense of patriotic duty and public service had remained with him to the very end. But Churchill concluded his eulogy on a more buoyant, optimistic and forward-looking note, leaving behind what he called 'the treasures of the past' and turning to what he felt certain, on the basis of past precedent, would be the glorious future that the new era of the second Elizabeth would now bring. 'Famous have been the reigns of our Queens,' he observed. 'Some of the greatest periods in our history have unfolded under their sceptres'; and there were two particular female monarchs from earlier times that were very much in his mind. One was the previous Queen Elizabeth: that 'magnificent figure who presided over and, in many ways, embodied ... the grandeur and genius' of the age to which she rightly gave her name. And the second, who defined and dominated her epoch with equal distinction and equal distinctiveness, was the sovereign who had occupied the imperial throne during the first twenty-seven years of Churchill's own life. He ended his broadcast, linking history and hope, times gone by with times yet to be: 'I, whose youth was passed in the august, unchallenged, tranquil glow of the Victorian era, may well feel a thrill in invoking once more the prayer and the anthem "God Save the Queen".'[1]

EUPHORIA

Thus the reign of Queen Elizabeth II began sixty years ago, which means that she is only the second British monarch of the modern era to celebrate her Diamond Jubilee, and that she is the only British monarch yet to complete the grand ceremonial and commemorative slam of a Silver, a Golden and a Diamond Jubilee. (There were no festivities in 1862 to mark the twenty-fifth anniversary of Queen Victoria's accession to the throne, since Prince Albert had died the previous year, and the first Silver Jubilee was that of King George V in 1935.) The precedent of Queen Victoria in 1897 is instructive in many ways for, as with all such occasions of precisely structured retrospection, it offered a vantage point from which to survey the sixty historic years that her Diamond Jubilee encompassed and celebrated. At the time, there was much for the British to feel proud of and grateful for: constitutional stability, democratic progress and increased prosperity at home across six decades and, during the same period, the extraordinary expansion of the greatest empire the world had ever known – an empire literally displayed on the streets of London, as potentates and troops appeared from all parts of the globe to pay homage to the sovereign. For the monarchy, this was also a remarkable period of transformation. At the beginning of Victoria's reign, it was not very rich, its ceremonial was often chaotic, its public standing uneven and uncertain, and its identification with empire little in evidence. But by 1897 its finances had improved, its ceremonial was spectacular, its popularity seemed adamantine, and the Queen had become as much an imperial icon as a national sovereign. Even though Rudyard Kipling's jubilee poem, 'Recessional', hinted at the mounting international and economic challenges that Britain faced as the nineteenth century drew to a close, and offered

a salutary reminder of the ephemerality of worldly power and the transience of imperial dominion, the celebrations of 1897 were undoubtedly the greatest show on the globe that year, and they were mounted by the nation that believed itself to be the greatest on earth, as its subjects rejoiced in one of the most sucessful periods in their history.

Despite the searing impact of the First and Second World Wars, the trauma of the abdication of King Edward VIII in 1936, and the end of the British Raj in India in 1947, the throne to which Queen Elizabeth II acceded in 1952 remained in many ways recognisably the same imperial institution that had been celebrated and acclaimed at the time of Queen Victoria's Diamond Jubilee. It was widely admired and esteemed, it was grand in its ceremonial and global in its reach, and as such it was a great-power monarchy that seemed entirely appropriate for the great-power nation that many believed and wanted Britain still to be. Indeed, by the early 1950s, Britain's was arguably the only upscale, world-class, high-end Crown that was surviving and thriving anywhere. In Europe, the Russian, German and Austro-Hungarian thrones had disappeared in 1917–18, while in Asia, the Chinese emperor and the Ottoman sultan had been overthrown before and immediately after the First World War; and although the Japanese emperor had survived his nation's defeat and devastation in 1945, he did so as a deeply discredited sovereign and much diminished figure. By contrast, the British monarchy was still very much a global, imperial, great-power institution, and Queen Elizabeth's Coronation was an appropriately global, imperial, great-power occasion. Regiments of colonial and Commonwealth troops once again marched on the streets of London, the prime ministers of the dominions and India were present in Westminster Abbey, princes and potentates from

Asia, Africa and the Pacific came to pay homage, and the successful conquest of Mount Everest by a British-led Commonwealth expedition, the news of which reached London on Coronation morning, was a triumphantly vindicating adventure at the very summit of the world. Thereafter, the Queen and Prince Philip departed on the recently commissioned Royal Yacht *Britannia* on a global, imperial, great-power progress, and they were rapturously received by vast and enthusiastic crowds, especially in Australia and New Zealand.

There cannot have been much of this that would have seemed strange to Queen Victoria – or, to be more precise, to the Queen Victoria of the later decades of her reign, for whether she knew it or not, whether she understood it or not, and whether she liked it or not, the imperial-ornamental British monarchy of which she herself became the epitome and embodiment, had been very much the creation of the last quarter of the nineteenth century, and it successfully survived and recognisably endured largely intact until the early 1950s. Nor would the Queen-Empress have been surprised or disappointed by the ringingly confident declaration that her great-great-granddaughter, Queen Elizabeth II, made towards the close of the day on which she had been crowned: 'I am sure that this, my Coronation, is not a symbol of a power and a splendour that are gone, but a declaration of our hopes for the future.'[2]

Despite these undoubted connections and continuities, it was not so much the precedents provided by Queen Victoria that caught the popular imagination at this time but, as Churchill's grandiloquent speech had hinted, the much more distant example of the first (as she now became known) Queen Elizabeth. During the early 1950s, there was much excited and euphoric talk of a 'second' or 'new Elizabethan age' that might be

Queen Victoria, cabinet card by W. & D. Downey, 1897

another golden era of national revival, overseas endeavour and unparalleled creativity. The timely conquest of Mount Everest lent credence to this view, and similar heroic deeds by a young generation of 'new Elizabethans', modelling themselves on the earlier, audacious examples provided by Sir Walter Ralegh and Sir Francis Drake, were eagerly anticipated. Meanwhile, to mark the Coronation year, British Railways revived the non-stop train service from London to Edinburgh, which was called 'The Elizabethan'.

RECESSIONAL

Although in many ways the throne Queen Elizabeth II inherited in 1952 was still a recognisably late-Victorian institution, and although the nation over which she reigned was one that retained late-Victorian pretensions to global greatness, the most pronounced themes that stand out across the sixty years of historic time that are marked by her

Queen Victoria
arriving for
the Diamond
Jubilee Service of
Thanksgiving at
St Paul's Cathedral,
1 January 1897

Diamond Jubilee are the de-Victorianisation and the downsizing of Britain and its empire, and also of the British monarchy. In the case of Britain and the empire, this retreat had already begun before 1952, as the defeat of Germany and Japan in 1945 had ushered in a politically polarised world order dominated by the United States and the Soviet Union, in which Britain was not only a lesser power than these American and Eurasian behemoths, but was also on the brink of economic ruin, depending for its very survival on American loans and Marshall Aid. All this had become clear during the crisis years of 1947–9, which witnessed the independence and partition of the Indian territories, the withdrawal of Britain from Palestine, the devaluation of the pound sterling, and an almost unendurably cold winter. These changes, and these diminutions, would alike be reflected in Queen Elizabeth II's title and in her Coronation, both of which, for all their

ostensible and substantive continuities with earlier times, were less imperial than those of her three predecessors. For Elizabeth II was neither Empress of India nor ruler of the British Dominions beyond the Sea, but merely Head of the Commonwealth. And despite the reverential television commentary provided by Richard Dimbleby, there were those who thought her Coronation was more about escapism and make-believe than about engaging with the diminished reality of Britain's post-war position. As one American journalist, H.V. Kaltenborn, insisted: 'this show [was] put on by the British for a psychological boost to their somewhat shaky empire'.[3]

Since the accession of Queen Elizabeth II, the downsizing of the British Empire and the de-Victorianisation of Britain have continued apace. (Or, to return to the other monarchical comparison often made at the time of her Coronation, the 'new Elizabethan age' proved to be a vain hope – the term soon became an embarrassment, and it rapidly disappeared.) In the early 1950s the British Empire still seemed to have some life and some future, but in 1957 Empire Day was replaced and superseded by Commonwealth Day, and by the end of the 1960s the empire had largely disappeared, to be replaced by a multiracial Commonwealth from which the adjective 'British' was significantly and symbolically removed. Three years after the Coronation, the Suez fiasco was an international humiliation, as the British failed to recover the Suez Canal, which Egypt's President Nasser had defiantly nationalised. This botched military operation made embarrassingly plain that Britain was a much-reduced force in the world, one that could no longer act independently, but only with the acquiescence and support of the United States. This retreat from great-power status continued during the Labour government led by Harold Wilson between 1964 and 1970, as Britain abandoned its military presence 'east of Suez' and as the pound was devalued yet again. Under his successor, Edward Heath, Britain turned away from the Commonwealth and what little was left of the empire, and joined the European Common Market. And for all Margaret Thatcher's subsequent claim to have reasserted Britain's global greatness in the aftermath of the Falklands War, she made no such attempt to defy China over the negotiations for the impending return of Hong Kong upon the expiration of Britain's lease. Fifty years after Indian independence, and one hundred years after Queen Victoria's Diamond Jubilee, the Hong Kong handover in 1997 marked the end of the British Empire and of imperial Britain, recessionals aptly symbolised by the presence of Prince Charles, who sailed away into the sunset on the final voyage of the Royal Yacht *Britannia*.

The great imperial power over which Queen Elizabeth II began to reign sixty years ago has largely disappeared, and today Britain is once again a middle-sized nation, having lost an empire while still trying to find its place, and to define its diminished position vis-à-vis Europe, the United States, the Commonwealth and the wider world. Meanwhile, and in addition to ceasing to be the imperial metropolis, the British nation itself has been significantly transformed within. As late as the early 1950s it remained in many ways a Victorian nation, not only internationally, but domestically too. Politically, the traditional, titled and territorial aristocracy had some life left in it, and some of its members continued to be socially close to the sovereign. The middle classes retained a strong imperial component, along with an ethos of military and civil service. And the working class was overwhelmingly employed in such nineteenth-century heavy industries as coal mining, the railways and steel production. Women knew their (subordinate) place, social mobility was limited, higher education was restricted to a tiny minority, while the influence of those who attended public schools and the universities of Oxford, Cambridge and London remained disproportionate. Britain was an ethnically homogeneous country, with few 'coloured' faces to be seen in the great cities, let alone the countryside. The Church of England and the Christian religion continued to be significant forces in both public and private life, shops were closed on Sundays and no sporting fixtures were held on the Sabbath, and the essentially Victorian moral code proscribed what were deemed to be such deviant practices and deplorable aberrations as homosexuality, divorce and abortion. Homosexuals could be, and often were, prosecuted; divorced personages were not accepted or welcomed at royal events, even if they were the innocent party; and

The Royal Coach travels along The Mall on the way from Buckingham Palace to Westminster Abbey for the Coronation of Queen Elizabeth II, 2 June 1953

abortion was illegal. Once again, Queen Victoria would not have found this world unfamiliar.

Domestically, as well as internationally, the overwhelming theme of the sixty years of the reign of Queen Elizabeth II has again been that of de-Victorianisation. The aristocracy has almost completely departed from the House of Lords and the corridors of power, leaving the monarchy more socially isolated than before; the imperial perspective and military ethos of the middle class have largely disappeared; and the de-industrialisation of Britain means that the same fate has overwhelmed the traditional, manual working class. A generally rising standard of living and the widening opportunities afforded by the unprecedented expansion of the higher education system have made Britain a more socially mobile and less deferential society, and the hegemony of public school and Oxbridge graduates is significantly less marked than it was. Since the 1950s, the influx of immigrants from the dissolving empire, especially from southern Asia,

Africa and the Caribbean, has transformed Britain into a more diverse population, while the decline of Christian observance means that there are now more practising Muslims than there are observant members of the Church of England. Today, and in a manner that had not been true during the reign of any previous sovereign, Britain is a multicultural, multi-ethnic, multi-faith society, where social inclusion is the conventional wisdom and aspiration, and where more foreign languages are spoken on the streets of London than in New York. During the 1960s, the youthful rebellions and student protests, combined with the reform of the laws concerning homosexuality, divorce and abortion, led to the discrediting and the dismantling of the Victorian moral code, with the result that today, same-sex unions are legal, divorce no longer spells social disgrace, and abortion has largely put an end to unwanted pregnancies. And the widespread use of birth control, combined with increased educational opportunities, means that women now occupy prominent and powerful positions in British public and professional life in a way that was unthinkable and unattainable during the early 1950s – unless you were the young woman who had inherited the British imperial throne as queen regnant.

ACCOMMODATION

The downsizing of its empire and the de-Victorianisation of Britain during the sixty years of the reign of Elizabeth II has been so pronounced that while the Queen-Empress Victoria would not have felt ill at ease in the imperial Britain that in so many ways survived until the early 1950s, she would have been amazed and baffled (and perhaps disappointed) by the post-imperial Britain that had both contracted and evolved by the early 2010s. That is in itself a vivid measure of the massive international and domestic changes that have taken place since the early 1950s, and that constitute the most significant and long-term themes of the present queen's reign. But what, meanwhile, has happened to the British monarchy during those same six decades? How has it responded to these unprecedented international and domestic changes? How far, in parallel and in step, has the House of Windsor de-Victorianised, de-imperialised and downsized? When Princess Elizabeth was born (with no realistic expectation of ever acceding to the throne), Queen Victoria had been dead scarcely twenty-five years, and the imperial British monarch was her grandfather, King George V, who was himself in many ways a quintessential late nineteenth-century figure. At that time, the British Empire encompassed one quarter of the land surface of the globe, and one quarter of the peoples of the world and, in accordance with earlier royal-imperial precedent, relatives of Princess Elizabeth would serve as Governor General of Canada, Australia and South Africa, while her cousin Lord Mountbatten would be appointed Viceroy of India. So it was hardly surprising that when she reached her twenty-first birthday in 1947, touring South Africa with her parents, King George VI and Queen Elizabeth, she publicly pledged that the whole of her life, be it long or short, would be spent in the service of the great empire-commonwealth to which she belonged – an undertaking made as the heiress presumptive to the imperial throne, and an undertaking that she subsequently renewed and reiterated as Queen Elizabeth II on the occasion of her Silver Jubilee in 1977.

By then, the British Empire and the British nation were very different entities from what they had been at the time of the Coronation, and the impact on the British monarchy was considerable. Royal tours to the Commonwealth became less ceremonial and more frequent, but as they became more routine,

they also became less resonant. Relations with the old dominions of Canada, Australia, New Zealand and South Africa were gradually loosening (indeed, South Africa withdrew from the Commonwealth in 1961 because other members objected to its racist policy of apartheid). In response to criticisms levelled in the late 1950s by the journalists John Grigg and Malcolm Muggeridge that the royal court was too stuffy and remote, the presentation of debutantes was ended, and the monarchy made an effort to adapt to what soon became known as the 'swinging sixties'. The Queen's sister, Princess Margaret, married a professional photographer, Antony Armstrong-Jones (later Lord Snowdon); her eldest son, Prince Charles, attended Gordonstoun School and the universities of Cambridge and Wales at Aberystwyth; and in 1969, the television film *Royal Family* offered an unprecedented glimpse into the public and private life of the Queen, Prince Philip and their children. But once (to borrow the political commentator Walter Bagehot's terms) this 'daylight' was let in on the 'magic', it could not be shut out, as an ever-more intrusive and less deferential press played up the breakdown of the marriage of Princess Margaret, and her subsequent divorce. The national mood, and the perception of the monarchy that was informed by it, were thus decidedly equivocal, uncertain and unsure at the time of the Queen's Silver Jubilee, which took place towards the end of the difficult and disillusioning decade of the 1970s. The pageantry, culminating in the 'traditional' Service of Thanksgiving at St Paul's Cathedral, was widely regarded as superb – something the British still did better than any other nation. But it was the first major royal spectacle that was also a post-imperial royal spectacle: 'there would only be a handful of troops from overseas to supplement the anyway modest British contingent; no foreign potentates … would lend exotic glamour to the proceedings'.[4]

Yet for all this contraction in the imperial reach of the British monarchy, and despite (or perhaps because of) the daylight that was increasingly being let in on the magic, it became clear during the next period of the Queen's reign that a credibility gap was opening up between the increasingly de-Victorianised, de-imperialised and downsized British nation and the insufficiently adjusted and attenuated British monarchy. At a time of recurrent economic crises, there was growing criticism of the cost of the royal family, a criticism intensified by the failed marriages of the Princess Royal, the Duke of York and the Prince of Wales, and by the proposal that the bill for repairing the fire damage to Windsor Castle in 1992 should be footed by the taxpayer. Although the rise in the rate of royal divorce mirrored the national trend, these failed marriages seriously undermined the belief that the royal family was also a happy family, and made the royal weddings in Westminster Abbey and St Paul's Cathedral seem, in retrospect, excessively ostentatious; while the more relaxed public manner of Diana, Princess of Wales, and the general decline in deferential attitudes, made the prevailing formal royal style seem cold, aloof and out of touch. It was no longer possible to send the sovereign's children overseas to be Governors General of the great dominions, and the Queen's tour to India in 1997, on the fiftieth anniversary of independence, engendered nationalist hostility more than it promoted Commonwealth friendship. The result was another recessional spurt of downsizing at the end of the 1990s: the Royal Yacht *Britannia* was given up, members of the royal family began to travel on public transport, the Queen agreed to pay tax on her private income, and Buckingham Palace was opened to paying visitors. The death of the Queen Mother, early in 2002, shortly before her daughter's Golden Jubilee, was a further landmark, for as the consort of the late King-Emperor George VI, she had also been the last Empress of India.

The ensuing Jubilee celebrations were relatively unostentatious and appropriately low key, and in a post-Diana world, they were planned to strike a more popular and inclusive tone. There were rock concerts in the gardens of Buckingham Palace (what would King George V or Queen Victoria have made of *that*?), and the celebrations around the Commonwealth were distinctly less grandiose or widespread then they had been around the British Empire in 1887. How, indeed, could – or should – it have been otherwise? In the same way, the Diamond Jubilee of 2012 cannot be – and should not be – expected to replicate the global spectacle of 1897, or the astonishing imperial tableaux that unfolded that year on the streets of London. Indeed, the less extravagant jubilees of 2002 and 2012, compared to those of 1887 and 1897, are a significant indication of the extent to which, during the present Queen's reign, the British Empire, the British nation and the British monarchy have significantly de-imperialised, de-Victorianised and downsized. This in turn means that the confident, expansive, onward and upward narratives that were triumphantly unfolded at the time of Queen Victoria's Golden and Diamond Jubilees cannot be replicated, and have not been replicated, for the corresponding celebrations of Queen Elizabeth II's reign. The monolithic empire story has been superseded by multiple Commonwealth narratives, which are more diverse, diffuse and dispersed, even though her continuing headship of the Commonwealth still gives the Queen a global position unique among today's monarchs. The British story is undeniably one of vanished great-power supremacy, but it is also a narrative of unprecedented opportunity and prosperity, and of the creation of a more open and more

tolerant society. As for the Queen herself, she is rightly acclaimed as the embodiment of lifelong duty and service, of stability and reassurance in a rapidly changing world, and as an essential link to earlier periods of historic greatness. This was scarcely the heroic future that had been ardently anticipated and eagerly looked forward to by Winston Churchill, by the 'new Elizabethans' and even by the young Queen during the early and euphoric 1950s, but nor, from the perspective of the second decade of the twenty-first century, are they trivial or inconsequential or insignificant accomplishments.

REPRESENTATION

It is often the illusion of contemporaries that they are living through a greater period of change than any that has previously occurred in human history. But there is a case to be made that the sixty years encompassed by the reign of Queen Elizabeth II have been remarkably transformative, and not just in the ways that have so far been depicted and described. Consider, in this regard, the innovations and the developments that have occurred in communications, the media and information technology, and their impact on the imaging and perception of royalty. During the years when Princess Elizabeth was growing up, there was portraiture, there was photography, there were newsreels and there was film. But as Queen Elizabeth II, she has had to deal with developments that none of her predecessors faced, especially the extraordinary impact of television during the first half of her reign, and of the information technology revolution during the second half. The small screen not only brought royal ceremonial into the homes of millions of people for the first time, but also made royal personages seem human and, in some cases, all too fallibly human. The era of twenty-four-hour global news, of multiple television channels, of social-networking sites and of instant imaging means that today the sheer quantity of visual information available about the British monarchy is greater than ever, more

The fly-past of twenty-seven aircraft, including the Red Arrows and Concorde, above The Mall as part of Queen Elizabeth II's Golden Jubilee celebrations, 4 June 2002

easily accessible and harder to regulate. From one perspective, these developments mean that the management of the Queen's media image has become an increasingly difficult, challenging and unrelenting task; but from another, they mean that Elizabeth II is probably the most visually depicted and represented individual ever to have existed across the entire span of human history. Indeed, who could her rivals be for that accolade, in the past or the present? She has been portrayed and photographed and filmed for the whole of her long life, she has been a global celebrity for sixty years on our television screens, and her Golden and Diamond Jubilees are the first such events to take place in the Internet age.

It is, then, particularly appropriate that the National Portrait Gallery is marking the Diamond Jubilee by examining representations of the Queen, both formal and informal, created throughout her reign. As such, they tell their own stories within and across those six decades, in terms of both the history of the monarchy and the history of the media. And these royal images must also be understood and interpreted in terms of the broader changes that have taken place in regard to the British Empire and the British nation, which have been briefly sketched out here. Yet it is also important to give appropriate attention to Elizabeth II herself, as an individual, as a woman, and above all as that relative rarity, a regnant queen. For the visual images and perceptions of female sovereigns have often been, and still are, very different from the visual images and perceptions of kingly men. The early photographs of Elizabeth II depicted her, appropriately, as a young and glamorous queen, and also as a happy and fulfilled mother. But middle-aged women, whether monarchs or Hollywood actresses or commoners, who are indeterminately positioned between youthful beauty and elderly grandmotherhood, tend to be less sympathetically depicted than middle-aged men. (Is it just coincidence that these were also the most difficult years in the reigns of both Queen Victoria and Queen Elizabeth I?) Moreover, the Queen was perceived and depicted as being middle-aged for a very long time. Early in 1953, and shortly before the Coronation, her grandmother, Queen Mary, the widow of King George V and the presiding matriarch of the House of Windsor, died. Thereafter, and for almost half a century, the next royal matriarch was the recently bereaved Queen Mother, and it was only on her death, just before her daughter's Golden Jubilee, that Queen Elizabeth II herself advanced from middle age to old age, by belatedly assuming the role and image of royal matriarch.

As these portraits of Queen Elizabeth II make plain, there is another, more positive, way of regarding and depicting a regnant queen. In earlier times, monarchs were rulers, and as such were essentially and generically male. They were gods or priests or lawgivers or judges or warriors or philosophers or patrons or benefactors, and they were accordingly portrayed as men of power. But in recent times, successfully surviving sovereigns have accommodated themselves to the increasingly democratic and egalitarian trends by ceasing to rule and by reigning instead. Albeit reluctantly during the time of Queen Victoria, the British royal house was the first great dynasty to undergo this change of function, and the phrase 'constitutional monarchy' was invented to describe (as Walter Bagehot put it) this 'dignified' rather than 'efficient' activity. In negative terms, constitutional monarchy may therefore be regarded as emasculated monarchy, with the ruling (and largely male) activities and justifications generally given up – which makes the depiction of male constitutional sovereigns, who are no longer men of power, something of a compositional challenge. But put more positively, this means that constitutional monarchy is in many ways a *feminised* monarchy, which makes it easier for a regnant queen to be sympathetically portrayed than a merely dignified king. Here is not only another way of understanding Queen Elizabeth II's long reign, but also of apprehending and appreciating the varied – and sometimes contradictory – images that, on the occasion of her Diamond Jubilee, not only record and celebrate sixty memorable and remarkable royal years, but also a great deal more besides.

[1] David Cannadine (ed.), *The Speeches of Winston Churchill* (London: Penguin, 1990), pp.316–19

[2] Conrad Frost, *Coronation: June 2 1953* (London: A. Barker, 1978), p.136

[3] Asa Briggs, *The History of Broadcasting in the United Kingdom: Volume IV: Sound and Vision* (Oxford: Oxford University Press, 1979), p.205

[4] Philip Ziegler, *Crown and People* (London: Collins, 1978), p.176

THE QUEEN: ART AND IMAGE

PAUL MOORHOUSE

In 2008, the fifty-sixth year of her reign, a striking, deeply unconventional image of Her Majesty The Queen was created by the contemporary artist Hew Locke. Born in Edinburgh in 1959, seven years after Queen Elizabeth II's accession to the throne, Locke was raised in Guyana. With the idea of Britishness as a central theme of his subsequent work, Locke chose to represent the ruling monarch of the United Kingdom and Head of the Commonwealth as Medusa (page 151). Comprising brightly coloured fragments of plastic, including beads, toys and other bits and pieces of discarded ephemera, Locke's sculpture interprets the Queen's image in ways that to some eyes may appear playful, but to others disrespectful. Drawing upon Greek myth, the reference to Medusa is, at the very least, deliberately provocative. Among the many implications advanced by this ambiguous, modern evocation of royalty, there is the disturbing suggestion that to gaze upon the face of the Queen is to be turned to stone.

Possibly even more unsettling is the realisation that Locke's distinctive assemblage shares its subject with a painting widely regarded as one of the greatest royal portraits of the twentieth century. Completed just over half a century earlier, in 1955, Pietro Annigoni's celebrated painting of the recently crowned Queen manifests an affecting sympathy with his sitter's presence and constitutional significance (page 69). The portrait sustains a compelling tension between dignity, regal splendour and a sensitive intimation of individuality. Annigoni successfully communicates a subtle sense of a human being inhabiting, but inseparable from, their public role.

The contrast between these respective images cannot, however, be explained simply in terms of differences in artistic temperament or attitude. The Annigoni was created two years after Elizabeth's Coronation, while the Locke anticipates her Diamond Jubilee, in 2012, by four years. The gulf that separates these works of art denotes nothing less than a sea change in the way the Queen is represented and perceived. The earlier portrait is formal and deferential; the more recent work appears to treat its subject as yet another disposable consumer product. Framing a period covering almost sixty years, such developments speak of fundamental shifts in the very strata of the society to which these images are addressed.

In order to understand the radical difference between these two modern evocations of royalty, it is necessary to explore what it is that unites them. Viewed in terms of their physical appearance, it would seem that the Annigoni and the Locke have little in common. At a deeper level, however, both artists are linked in terms of a shared, fundamental endeavour. Despite the apparent incompatibility of their respective approaches, Annigoni and Locke both responded to the same subject – the Queen – through the creation of an image. Although Annigoni painted his portrait from life while Locke constructed his response from found detritus, both resulting works of art have the status of being a pictorial representation of their shared subject. In the absence of the sitter, a sense of physical presence and the intimation of certain characteristics are evoked by the surrogate reality of the portrait or assemblage. As images, therefore, both are rooted, essentially, in artifice.

Although artificial, no image is ever entirely mute. To a greater or lesser degree, every visual representation conveys information not only about its subject, but also about the circumstances of its making. From the values and intentions of its creator to the social conditions that determined its particular appearance, as the adage informs us: 'every picture tells a story'. This maxim is particularly true when applied to images of the Queen. It is likely that, since her birth in 1926, Elizabeth has been portrayed more frequently than any other sitter in history (see left, one of the many photographs of the Queen taken by Cecil Beaton) and, during the sixty years of her reign, this process has intensified and diversified. Her image forms the basis for formal painted portraits, studio photographs, innumerable photographs reproduced in magazines and newspapers, extensive film footage, stamps and currency, an astonishing range of ephemera, as well as a burgeoning response by contemporary artists working in a variety of different media. Given the vast range of ways to represent the Queen, it is not surprising to discover a concomitant diversity in terms of the quality of

the results. But even a modest overview yields a single impression: that of an enduring individual whose presence is immediate yet also elusive. Instantly recognisable, the Queen nevertheless remains an enigmatic figure. Familiar to most, she is known only to a few, and her thoughts and opinions on many subjects remain undisclosed.

This book and the accompanying exhibition chart a path through that complex, richly textured terrain of images. Initially, the sheer expanse of material appears bewildering, as if any possibility of a coherent iconography has been thrown into disarray by the competing imperatives of tradition and modernity. Formal portraiture, the demands of the media and the uninhibited responses of contemporary artists all yield apparently divergent perspectives. However, exploring this territory reveals certain clear, if surprising, lines of development. Among these is the furrow cut by a progressive interaction between formal portraiture and the mass media. While in the 1950s portraitists

such as Annigoni seemed to occupy a world apart from that of the news photographer, in a modern, image-saturated society such distinctions could not be maintained indefinitely. In the last sixty years, the evolution of representations of the Queen has been characterised by a dialogue between traditional portraiture and the world of newspapers, magazines and television. The resulting informality galvanised the work of contemporary artists such as Gerhard Richter, Andy Warhol, Gilbert and George, Lucian Freud, Annie Leibovitz and Hew Locke. In their different ways, each appropriated, manipulated and reinvented the Queen's image, producing a new iconography that has reflected and influenced fresh perceptions of royalty. Set within a wider, social context, these manifold representations of the monarch provide a lens through which her reign may be viewed. Such contemporary reimaginings also evoke a resonant social, historical and artistic context.

The question therefore arises as to what all these different, changing images can tell us. The answer is somewhat paradoxical – for this heterogeneous pictorial field both reveals a great deal and retains much besides. Creating an image of any individual immediately poses a question about the veracity of the relationship between the subject and the depiction. An image or portrait creates an appearance, implying not only physical details but also intimations of character, mood and context. The extent to which this appearance corresponds with the reality it depicts remains a matter for conjecture and, after a period of time has elapsed, an image may increasingly be open to interpretation. Indeed, the reliability of some pictorial representations, including photographs, may be forever unverifiable. When these issues involve the Queen, their complexities are manifold.

A central question relates to her role. Apart from private instances shared with intimate family and friends, the Queen is a public figure whose presence is usually viewed within the context of display. That this is so on ceremonial or formal occasions is self-evident. In such instances as her Coronation or the State Opening of Parliament, the Queen's appearance and presence had, and have, a symbolic significance. But even when she has been captured in a non-formal situation, notably when the 1969 film *Royal Family* included extensive behind-the-scenes footage of family occasions, it is uncertain whether such glimpses show the private individual or whether these too are a form of display for public consumption (pages 46 and 89). The role of the sovereign involves being subjected to scrutiny, and while this outward-facing persona may be an extension of the private individual, it would be a gross simplification to assume that the private person and the public figure are identical. Being the Queen, to some extent, involves inhabiting a role, the outward appearance of which is the regal image.

The image of the Queen is not confined to pictorial representation. Rather, it is primarily an abstract idea embodying certain values made apparent, and given substance, in the reality of the public situations in which she is physically present. To see the Queen is to make immediate contact with the image of royalty. Nor is this limited to ceremonial occasions. In recent years, the Queen's image has been 'softened' by her appearance in informal encounters in ordinary settings – for example, when visiting members of the public in their own homes (page 133). However, even without the trappings of state, the context of her role leaves no room for doubt as to her position and what she represents. Whatever the public occasion, the Queen remains a figure apart, a characteristic acknowledged even by her detractors.

The way the Queen is presented is of critical importance in sustaining her image, and this in turn supports the special status that she retains. It is for this reason that so much attention has been paid during the course of her reign to the question of how she is perceived, how this public perception has changed, and how her image may be adapted to meet the changing demands of a continually evolving society. This is an ongoing process that has engaged the Queen's own officials, the royal family, the machinery of government, historians, social commentators, journalists and the public. Significantly, all these constituencies have been, and continue to be, involved in shaping the idea, role and image of the Queen. To this list could also be added abstractions such as tradition – whether real or invented[1] – the notion of which remains a potent element in the creation of the Queen as an institution.

The Queen may be familiar to millions around the globe but, like most famous individuals, for the man or woman in the street she is seen from afar. The impressions of her present in the minds of ordinary people are not based on reality, but on innumerable virtual representations. The royal image is therefore not simply an abstraction made apparent during public display. Instead, a further, even more complicated, layer of visual information exists in the form of formal portraits, photographs taken for purposes of documentation or news, and contemporary art works. These manifestations mediate and transmit the Queen's image to a vast international audience.

Depictions of royalty have a long historical pedigree. The earliest royal portraits, both in the form of paintings and as coinage, were created and copied to disseminate an image or idea of the reigning monarch. In that respect, representing the Queen pictorially is nothing new. But in the last sixty years, the vast proliferation of images of the Queen, in all media, has surpassed historical antecedents. Also unique to the recent past is the manner in which such imagery has not only diversified but also cross-fertilised. The result of this interaction has been nothing less than a revolution in the way the Queen is represented and perceived. The nature of that revolution, unfolding from 1952 to 2012, is the subject of the present essay.

FORMALITY TO FAMILIARITY

From the moment of her accession, the Queen has been subjected to an extraordinary barrage of relentless visual scrutiny. She has sat for numerous formal portraits, including royal commissions requested from public and charitable institutions. Created by an array of artists, the results form a fascinating, often distinguished, and highly diverse extension of a royal portrait tradition. From James Gunn working in 1953–4 (page 38) to Lucian Freud in 1999–2001 (page 139), each portraitist brings a different perception. The result has been a range of interpretations with varying degrees of success, both in terms of quality and apparent insight. Despite this diversity, such formal portraits have a common aim: to make an image of the Queen that will, in some deeper sense, speak to perpetuity.

Closely linked to these painted images has been a corresponding lineage of formal, studio-based photographic portraits. In this respect too the Queen has been served by many outstanding practitioners, from Dorothy Wilding (pages 57 and 59) and Cecil Beaton (pages 61 and 64) in the 1950s, to compelling contributions in recent years from Annie Leibovitz (page 152) and Chris Levine (pages 143 and 149). Such images are no less exacting in terms of the photographers' shared aim of preserving a likeness. Many, such as Beaton's Coronation photograph of 1953 (page 61), have an iconic significance that rivals more traditional painted portraits. In addition, formal photographs have been used in a variety of contexts, notably as official images for formal distribution, as personal gifts and greetings cards, as the basis for stamps and currency, as well as for use by a voracious international press.

Concurrent with the production of these studio-based portraits, the Queen has been observed and her image recorded by another constituency whose purpose and methods differ from those of formal portraitists, but whose impact as royal image-makers is no less significant. The mass-media boom, which gathered momentum from the 1960s, fostered an expansion in the ranks of photographers whose work is directed solely towards reproduction in the press. Although magazines such as *Vogue* have, since the early twentieth century, provided a platform for images of royalty, the emergence of a more widely disseminated popular culture during the 1960s sustained even greater visibility in terms of the Queen's appearance and activities. This growing media exposure was underpinned by the expansion and subsequent ubiquity of television, a process that was given a significant boost at the outset by popular interest in the Queen. Anticipating the Coronation, the number of television licence holders doubled to three million in 1952. Since the 1980s, largely in response to unprecedented press interest in Princess Diana and the royal family generally, the media has continued to be an energetic conduit for images of the Queen.

It says a great deal about contemporary society that in recent years many of the most telling representations of the Queen have been press images. Whereas formal royal portraits aim to have lasting interest, photographs of the Queen produced for newspapers aim for a more immediate effect, eschewing posterity. They seek to capture a fleeting moment that is reported as news. In this context, there is a notable photograph of the Queen and Prince Philip surveying floral tributes after the tragic death of Diana, Princess of Wales (page 129). Reproduced in *The Times* on 5 September 1997, it recorded a fleeting instant. Yet among contemporary representations this is a telling image that depicts the Queen at a critical moment in her reign. For that reason, its significance and value are unlikely to be diminished by the passage of time.

In their very different ways, formal portraits of the Queen and photographs and film footage created for use in the media each play a vital role in shaping the image and perception of the monarch. In the case of studio-based images, this shaping process is to some extent conscious and deliberate. It is also a response to influences whose origins may not always be obvious. Annigoni's second painted portrait of 1969 (page 91), for example, was a personal response to the regal image he had first encountered in his previous sittings with the Queen fifteen years earlier (page 69). On both occasions his observations were the product of many factors.

The Queen's formal and symbolic role; the advice and support of her family, courtiers and advisers; the sovereign's personal sense of her position, subsequently deepened by age; her individual perception of history and tradition; her own views on how a modern monarch should be seen: all these elements, and many others, contributed to creating the persona. In turn, the artist responded to a complex array of impressions, producing a representation of an individual that is deeply nuanced, coloured by his own understanding and perceptions. In translating these subjective experiences into paint, a sense of context also played an inevitable role. Any image is informed by the time and atmosphere in which it is created. In creating a royal portrait, the values and expectations of a public audience are not the least of the many significant factors that play a part in its conception and realisation.

By contrast, photographic images that appear in the media are less directed, less susceptible to control. A formal portrait may often admit a degree of communion between the sitter and the painter or photographer who responds. Both sides of this equation share, to some degree, a sense of intention about the impression they wish to convey, whether this is rooted in likeness and appearance or in transmitting more symbolic values. This is much less the case with media images. Like other forms of reportage, photographs of the Queen taken spontaneously in a public setting are inherently responsive rather than directed to a particular end. A press photographer is presented with the

Queen in a particular setting. This may involve all kinds of factors relating to the location as well as to other participants. Outside the controlled situation provided by the Yellow Drawing Room at Buckingham Palace (the usual venue for portrait sittings), neither the Queen nor the photographer will be able entirely to dictate the flow of events. The light at a certain moment, an unforeseen occurrence, a particular expression: all contribute or conspire to create an unpredictable result.

Whereas at the beginning of the Queen's reign Fleet Street could be relied upon to exercise discretion, in recent years an increasing sense of freedom to reproduce whatever is deemed newsworthy has become the norm for many newspapers. Press images of the Queen may or may not support the impression desired by the subject of this attention. Yet, significantly, the way the Queen has been portrayed in the media has been enormously influential in forming the image that the public has of her. While it was assumed that formal portraits to some extent sustain artifice, press photographs have increasingly probed the fracture between the public persona and the private individual. It is for this reason that the photographs depicting the Queen's response to the devastation by fire of Windsor Castle in 1992 carry a particular frisson (page 127). They suggest that, for a moment, any royal façade has slipped, exposing a more immediate reality.

The currency of such images of the Queen reveals much about a society that, in the space of sixty years, has shifted its allegiance from formality to familiarity. In place of the trappings of state, exposed human emotion has been admitted, as if providing a greater seal of authenticity. In this way, an alternative view of the Queen has been presented by an increasingly intrusive press. This is image-making geared less to deference than to

revelation, as if the mystique of royalty is being deconstructed. Indeed, since the 1960s many photographers have progressively stripped away the formal and symbolic attributes of the Queen's image, replacing these with portraits that instead emphasise a more relaxed, approachable monarch. Eve Arnold (page 86), Patrick Lichfield (page 97), Snowdon (page 105) and Norman Parkinson (page 109) led this process, gradually producing a new evocation of royalty that is warmer and more down-to-earth.

These developments have posed questions that for so long were not so much unspoken as not even contemplated. However, a rapidly changing society made such imponderables inescapable. For example, in 1964 a Mass Observation survey revealed that 60 per cent of the British population were 'entirely favourable' towards royalty.[2] By 1994, this figure had declined to 29 per cent. Of those surveyed, 54 per cent felt that the royal family should continue, but needed to be more democratic and approachable.[3] The new generation of informal royal photography was in accord with the general movement towards greater approachability. Presenting the gap between monarchy and ordinary life as having narrowed, the question encapsulated by such images is a fundamental one. In a more democratic society, less tolerant of formal privileged status, it relates to the very purpose of having a monarch.

Such developments towards greater informality have also been a potent influence on contemporary artists for whom the image of the Queen and the idea of royalty have been subjects rich in potential for exploration and reinvention. Associated with convention, the Queen may seem an unlikely, even unpromising, subject for artists whose work by its very nature challenges the status quo. However, artists working in freer, more experimental and imaginative ways may be seen as responding to the

ongoing dialogue between formal portraiture and the more informal view of the Queen presented by the mass media. From the 1960s an international array of artists, including Gerhard Richter (pages 80 and 83), Andy Warhol (pages 119–22), Gilbert and George (pages 111–12) and, more recently, Hiroshi Sugimoto (page 135) and Chris Levine (pages 143 and 149), have in different ways each probed questions concerning the Queen's image. At the heart of their highly individual responses has been a concern with what a modern monarch stands for and how the Queen should be perceived. Underpinning both these issues is the critical question of how to represent the Queen. In an age that has energetically dismantled the machinery of deference, what should royalty look like?

In common with much earlier formal royal portraiture, James Gunn's state portrait of the Queen painted in 1953–4 (left) advances an inescapable sense of artifice. This was the veneer that modern press photographs of the Queen have largely shattered. A brittle surface evoking exalted status has been replaced with something that more closely resembles the familiar features of ordinary life. The question this raised, however, was the veracity of the new, informal image of the monarch. From that uncertainty flowed a new anxiety. Can the Queen be ordinary yet remain, by virtue of her position, somehow still exalted and above the everyday? If so, what is the relationship between these two apparently irreconcilable aspects? Having witnessed the deconstruction of the formal image of royalty, contemporary artists have engaged with those issues that have arisen, as it were, from the wreckage. Their imperative has been to investigate the modern dilemma posed by an individual inhabiting the historic role of queen. At the heart of that endeavour has been a new engagement with the Queen's image.

Any form of artistic representation presents a vital point of contact between those responsible for its creation and those who perceive it. For that reason, the huge diversity of images of the Queen produced since her accession to the throne are a rich source of information, not only about how the Queen has been presented, but also about the changing times that are their context. Viewed over sixty years, certain evolving preoccupations are apparent. The first and earliest period, from 1952 to the mid-1960s, reflects a concern with the young Queen's appearance. The second, corresponding approximately to the late 1960s to early 1980s, demonstrates a new concern with reinventing the sovereign's public image. The third phase, covering the last thirty years, manifests an ongoing engagement with the question of what the Queen represents.

LIKENESS

It is significant that the process of constructing the public persona of Queen Elizabeth II began not with the trappings of state and symbolism associated with formal portraiture but, rather, with a photograph taken, it seems, without her being aware of it. On 7 February 1952 the new Queen was photograped at London Airport (page 56). Elizabeth is shown standing at the centre of a group of people that had assembled to meet her on the tarmac. This included the Prime Minister Winston Churchill, the Leader of the Opposition Clement Attlee, Lord and Lady Mountbatten and other dignitaries. News of the death of her father, King George VI, had reached Princess Elizabeth while she was on tour with Prince Philip in Kenya, and in London a swiftly convened Accession Council proclaimed the new monarch. The press photograph shows her at the moment of her return to British soil, dressed in black, looking sombre and somewhat diminutive. Although understated, this image records a turning point in Elizabeth's life and the opening of a new chapter in recent history.

From the outset, attention focused on the Queen's appearance. Published photographs of royalty were not new. The Coronation of George V and Queen Mary in 1911 had featured in the pages of the press, and royal features were a staple of magazines from the early 1920s. However, from the moment that Elizabeth's destiny as a future queen became apparent, there was a new, deeper fascination with her physical allure. As early as 1947, she was described in the press as 'unquestionably the most publicised young woman in the world'.[4] Around the same time, her private secretary Jock Colville noted her 'beautiful blue eyes and superb natural complexion'.[5] After her accession, Cecil Beaton referred to 'the

purity of her expression'[6] and, although initially cautious about her lack of experience, Churchill was won over, identifying her freshness with 'a new Elizabethan Age'.[7] This appeal, and the way it translated readily in visual terms, is evident in the captivating photographs taken by Dorothy Wilding in 1952 (pages 57 and 59). To mark her accession, the Queen posed for Wilding fifty-nine times, wearing evening gowns designed by Norman Hartnell. Subsequently, copies of the best photographs were sent to every embassy in the world. They also formed the basis of designs on banknotes and appeared on millions of stamps. Youth and beauty were central to the image that began to take shape.

This emphasis on public visibility was at the heart of the thinking behind the Coronation, which took place on 2 June 1953 (pages 33 and 60). The crowning of a monarch is an event steeped in constitutional and religious significance, heavy with symbolism relating to sacrifice, duty, responsibility, national unity and history. For the first time ever, this historic occasion became available to the gaze of millions. Broadcast by the BBC, the procession, service and crowning were seen by an estimated twenty-seven million television viewers in Britain alone.[8] At the centre of this attention, the twenty-six-year-old Elizabeth captivated the collective imagination of observers around the world, as well as lighting up a country in which post-war food rationing did not cease until the following year.

Afterwards, the Queen travelled to Buckingham Palace to be photographed by Cecil Beaton in the Picture Gallery (page 61). In the resulting Coronation photograph the Queen is shown wearing the Imperial State Crown and her Coronation Robes. The Coronation Gown, designed by Norman Hartnell, is embroidered with emblems of the United Kingdom and the

Commonwealth. She holds the Orb and Sceptre, and on the third finger of her right hand the Coronation Ring is visible. Behind her can be seen a large-scale photograph of the interior of the Chapel of Henry VII at Westminster Abbey. This backdrop lends Beaton's photograph an imposing grandeur. But the inherent artifice of this elaborate piece of staging also conveys a strange ambiguity. This formal image, the defining visual record of the last monarch to be crowned in Britain in the twentieth century, is both impressive and strangely unreal. Not for the last time, the actual, the symbolic and the apparent would make an uneasy alliance in an image of the Queen.

The powerful impression created by these televised and formal images of the young Queen contributed to the unprecedented general adulation that followed. While her father and grandfather had inspired national affection, fascinated admiration was a new sentiment to be associated with royalty. Nor was this perception confined to the United Kingdom. In November 1953 the Queen and Prince Philip commenced an extensive tour of the Commonwealth. The focus of the tour, which lasted five and a half months, was New Zealand and Australia, although the young royals also made visits to numerous countries in the Caribbean, Africa and the Mediterranean. Throughout, the Queen was a highly visible presence, attending numerous formal functions and maintaining a punishing schedule of public appearances. As an exercise in projecting the Queen's image abroad, it was hugely successful, cementing international regard and a sense of unity within the evolving Commonwealth.

Almost immediately, the way the Queen was perceived began to undergo a subtle but significant transformation. Those qualities of youth, freshness, beauty and purity that had first registered with observers now acquired a deeper, symbolic

significance. In an age still bearing the scars of a recent, costly and devastating international war, and now beset by ongoing anxieties about the threat of nuclear conflict, the Queen was seen as a ray of hope. As ever, Churchill had sensed the national mood and given it direction. Even before the Coronation, he had held out the prospect that 'a fair and youthful figure … may be the signal for such a brightening salvation of the human scene'.[9] In this way the Queen was seen as the embodiment of the future, symbolising renewal and growth. It was not long before political commentators and, in their wake, public opinion began to extend this symbolism to the wider population. Within two years of the Coronation, *The Times* commented: 'Now in the twentieth-century conception of the monarchy the Queen has come to be the symbol of every side of life of this society, its universal representative in whom her people see their better selves ideally reflected …'[10] No longer simply an object of admiration, the image of the monarch now became identified with wider social values.

This idealised view of the Queen found superlative expression in the remarkable portrait painted for the Fishmongers' Company by Pietro Annigoni in 1954–5 (page 69). The product of fifteen sittings that took place between October and Christmas 1954, Annigoni's image is a profound distillation of different perceptions. The Queen is represented against a romantic landscape, a deep, recessive space that surrounds the figure, wrapping it in an aura of solitude. Yet the atmosphere created by the painter and sitter is not one of introspection. The Queen's expression is at once alert and observant, as if surveying her surroundings. It is this fusion of isolation and connectedness that accounts for the peculiar fascination exercised by the portrait. It is an image that seems to speak not only of the sitter's presence but of her relation to the world. At a deeper level, Annigoni struck a chord in the nation's sense of itself. The Queen seemed to represent an island people, dignified and alone, yet outward-looking and compassionate.

However, public opinion is fickle and forever influenced by events. The Suez crisis of 1956 presented Britain in a new, discreditable light. The British response to the Egyptian nationalisation of the Suez Canal Company, which it part-owned with France, was to bomb Egyptian airfields. This perceived aggression resulted in a run on the pound and, after being refused help by the Americans, the Prime Minister, Anthony Eden, was forced to accept a ceasefire arranged by the UN. Britain emerged from this fiasco damaged, no longer able to maintain her earlier imperial superpower status. In the same way that favourable connections had been made between the Coronation and the simultaneous conquest of Mount Everest, now adversity coincided with criticism of the Queen. The world and Britain's place within it seemed to many to be changing. Having written in 1955 that the public may 'feel that another photograph of the Royal Family will be more than they can bear',[11] the journalist Malcolm Muggeridge observed in 1957 that: 'The impulses out of which snobbishness is born descend from the Queen.' He added: 'If it is considered … that such a social set-up is obsolete and disadvantageous in the contemporary world, then the Monarchy is to that extent undesirable.'[12] Society was changing, but in different ways and at different speeds. If *The Times* had been correct in portraying the Queen as the 'symbol of every side of life', then a changing world meant that negotiating an appropriate image was now going to be much more complex.

For the immediate future, a workable and effective theme was the way the Queen was seen through images that emphasised her position as a mother and as the embodiment of family

life. A photograph published in *The Times* on 27 December 1957 shows the Queen's face on a television screen (page 73). She is at the centre of a family group watching the first-ever televised broadcast of the Christmas Day address, a regular event in British life since the practice had been started by the Queen's grandfather, George V, on the radio in 1932. Other photographs of the Queen taken in the late 1950s and throughout the 1960s carry a similar domestic message. In 1957 Antony Armstrong-Jones, later Lord Snowdon, created an intimate and touching evocation of royal family life (page 70). Taken in the garden of Buckingham Palace, the Queen and Prince Philip are seen on a bridge looking down at their children, Prince Charles and Princess Anne. Following the birth of her third child, Prince Andrew, on 19 February 1960, an even more intimate view of the Queen was presented in a photograph by Cecil Beaton that dwells, in close-up, on the relation of mother and infant (page 77). A further photograph by Beaton, taken in 1964, shows the Queen, the three-year-old Prince Andrew and a newly born Prince Edward (page 76).

Alongside these glimpses of royal domesticity, a parallel stream of newspaper images and formal photographs maintained their earlier allegiance to the Queen's public role. In 1961, the Queen and Prince Philip undertook a six-week tour of the Indian subcontinent, including visits to Nepal, India and Pakistan. A memorable photograph taken in Delhi depicts the Queen from behind as she addresses an audience, her largest to date, that stretches to the horizon (page 78). The contrast with the images of family life could not be more striking. Even so, all these documentary portraits are linked in conveying an impression of Elizabeth's role in embodying family values. The private photographs do this overtly, presenting the

Queen Elizabeth II
by Yousuf Karsh, 1966

Queen as a mother. Such images are a reassuring confirmation of the royal family and the Queen in particular as symbols of ordinary British life. The photograph of the Queen in Delhi has a more subtle significance. It presents her as a public figure, but one who brings together, and provides a focus for, the extended family represented by Britain's ties with the wider, post-empire, English-speaking world. The relationship of people, embodied by the Queen, is the theme of both these iconographical issues. That said, in the case of the Delhi photograph, the sense of unity that it implies is more metaphorical than actual. Avoiding any implication of continued royal authority, India's invitation to visit was addressed to the Queen of the United Kingdom and not to the Head of the Commonwealth.

Whether embodying private family life or providing a focus for the wider family of peoples, the Queen's image was not immune to changes in the way she was perceived as the

1960s unfolded. The photographs of the Queen taken by Yousuf Karsh in 1966 are undeniably compelling in their evocation of sumptuous elegance and cool dignity (left and page 79). They reveal a monarch now mature, confident and established in her position. However, they can be seen as an antidote to diminishing public interest. The popular perception of the Queen remained positive. Notwithstanding critics such as Muggeridge, she remained popular, and criticism was muted. That said, with growing familiarity, the media's level of interest in the Queen had dropped away significantly. The sense of glamour that was an integral part of the image presented at the beginning of her reign had been replaced by something more dependable. Karsh's photographs are a powerful reminder of regal splendour. However, in some ways they represent the end of an image that had served the monarch in the 1950s, a decade more attuned to formal privilege.

In the context of the social revolution enacted in the 1960s, the issue confronting the Queen was that she looked dangerously out of date. With a progressive dismantling of established social hierarchies, the splendour of exalted status looked less appealing, and less relevant, than more authentic everyday reality. From the mid-1960s a number of artists and photographers began to explore, in their different ways, some radical departures from received royal image-making. Collectively, these works demonstrate the flowering of an extraordinary new willingness – and a freedom – to investigate new ways of representing royalty.

IMAGE

On Friday 21 October 1966 the mining community at Aberfan near Merthyr Tydfil in South Wales was devastated by a human tragedy of appalling proportions. Without warning, an enormous colliery waste heap slid down a mountainside into the village, engulfing a junior school and twenty homes. One hundred and forty-four people died, of whom one hundred and sixteen were children. Both Prince Philip and the Prime Minister, Harold Wilson, visited the disaster area immediately, but the Queen hesitated. The growing public perception was that the Queen's presence was needed, and nine days later she made a tour, meeting local families and people (right). This simple gesture was welcomed but, with hindsight, the preceding pause was significant. It seemed to signal a potential distance from ordinary life and the imperative reality of human emotions. Suddenly, images of the Queen that emphasised the extraordinary, elevated nature of her role seemed out of touch with a world in which media-generated pictures of human suffering were ever present.

A fast-changing world presented very real difficulties for an institution rooted in a sense of continuity, stability and predictability. Presented in the pages of newspapers and magazines and through the medium of television, the Queen had reached an audience the size of which far outstripped that of her predecessors. But the price of this vastly expanded access was a growing familiarity and, among some sections of the public, a resulting indifference. It was noticeable that her public appearances no longer generated the earlier sense of anticipation or excitement. However, it was equally apparent that actively projecting an image of special status was no longer an option. As the Aberfan episode had showed, it seemed a more down-to-earth, common touch was needed to suit the mood of the time.

Two images of the Queen created around this time by the German artist Gerhard Richter encapsulate this uncertainty. In common with

The Queen at Aberfan
by Stan Meagher,
30 October 1966

all Richter's figurative work, both are based on photographs that the artist manipulated in various ways. The first, a lithograph made in 1966, depicts the Queen in close-up (page 80). Derived from a newspaper image, it shows her outdoors, wearing a large hat. However, Richter deliberately blurred the original photograph. The resulting print seems out of focus. Its subject lacks definition, frustrates explanation and is difficult to read. Richter followed this view of an elusive Queen with a painting, made the following year, which presents a starkly contrasted evocation of the same subject (page 83). Here, a photograph of the Queen has been transposed in paint through the use of lurid colour. Rather than remote, the motif has an exaggerated, artificially enhanced presence; one that is both insistent and entirely ambiguous.

Depicting the Queen in this way was an extraordinary development. Earlier formal portraits, such as those by Gunn and Annigoni, manifest a reverential and respectful response. Richter's view of his royal sitter is neither deferential nor disrespectful. Instead, it is simply equivocal. Richter's images appear qualified, inscrutable and deliberately uncertain. Without declaring a definable position, these very qualities appear to be a comment on his subject matter. The Queen emerges as an enigma, a perception completely at one with her predicament at that moment.

A similar quality of mystery, albeit realised in very different terms, pervades Annigoni's second portrait of the Queen, commissioned by the Trustees of the National Portrait Gallery and organised by the art dealer Sir Hugh Leggatt, which the artist completed in 1969 (page 91). Annigoni had been the Queen's own choice for the commission, but if a predictable outcome was expected, this was not to be the case. The product of ten months' work and eighteen sittings, the portrait returns to those themes set out in the earlier painting. Previously, the artist had perceived in his sitter's youthful presence a dignified – if slightly unapproachable – sensuality. He now represented an older monarch, still isolated by her position, but occupying a void, without recognisable points of reference. Annigoni explained: 'I did not want to paint her as a film star; I saw her as a monarch, alone in the problems of her responsibility.'[13] These words are prescient, for they signal a reaction against the impression of glamour that had coloured the public's perception of the Queen during the early part of her reign. Without ingratiating superficial physical appeal, Annigoni's Queen retains a quiet dignity. But there is a palpable absence of familiar landmarks in a changing world.

As the second Annigoni portrait seems to imply, by the late 1960s a glamorised view of the Queen was no longer appropriate. Nor, as recent events showed, was she still the focus of rapt admiration.

As early as 1963, dissent had been voiced during a public appearance in London with the King and Queen of Greece. At the time of Aberfan the Queen's absence had been questioned. In 1968, during a visit to the University of East Anglia, there were student protests. The growing realisation was that her continued relevance required a new relationship with a more vocal public.

In 1968–9, there is the visual evidence of a dramatic shift in the terms of that relationship as the Queen began to be presented in a different light. Stiff formality was replaced with a renewed emphasis on the Queen's qualities as a human being. Eve Arnold's photograph of the Queen sheltering underneath the umbrella she is holding is both refreshingly informal and startlingly spontaneous (page 86). As if snapped by a casual observer, the Queen is shown wearing daytime clothes. Apparently caught unawares by a sudden shower, she is staring at the sky and smiling. Most remarkable, given that Arnold's subject is the monarch, is the way the entire image conveys a sense of light-hearted, relaxed ordinariness. This is not to suggest that the Queen had not been photographed 'off duty' on earlier occasions. Studio Lisa had photographed the Queen, dressed in a tweed jacket, in the grounds of Frogmore, Windsor in 1959 (opposite). But that very appealing earlier image has a studied informality absent in Arnold's photograph. The Studio Lisa portrait presents the Queen in a relaxed situation. By contrast, the Arnold could be a glimpse of an ordinary member of the public.

The idea of an 'ordinary' sovereign may appear to be a contradiction in terms and, at the very least, creating an appropriate image of this hybrid concept would be a difficult balancing act. However, responsive to the feeling among the Queen's advisers that a more contemporary view of the monarch was needed, royal assent to take positive action in that direction was granted. Television was recognised as being the most effective medium for disseminating this new look to a wide audience. The result was the documentary film *Royal Family*, directed by Richard Cawston in a joint production by Independent Television (ITV) and BBC Television (pages 46 and 89). It was described by the makers as 'a filmed portrait of Queen Elizabeth II and her family – on and off duty'.[14] As this encapsulation suggests, the producers secured unprecedented permission to film the Queen and members of her family both in their formal operations and behind the scenes, in unrehearsed moments of informal behaviour. The result was a ninety-minute feature compiled from footage covering a year in the life of the royal family. Transmitted twice in June 1969, first by the BBC and subsequently by ITV, it quickly received several repeats, reaching a total audience that far outstripped that even for the Coronation.

In terms of the public's evolving perception of the Queen, and indeed of royalty generally, Cawston's film represents a landmark achievement. To an extent previously thought unimaginable, the effect of seeing the monarch and her family talking and behaving as individuals, unconstrained by the formalities of public occasion, was a revelation. A critical as well as a popular success, *Royal Family* irreversibly changed the way the Queen was regarded. That said, whether the picture that was presented – of ordinary life behind the façade of formal duty – was reliable or simply another layer of representation, remained a matter for conjecture. The issue of veracity aside, the immediate, observable consequence of the film was to present the Queen and her family in an entirely new light and one that seemed to relate more meaningfully to the general public.

In the longer term, the truthfulness – or not – of the new royal image would test its capacity to survive a period of turbulent social change. For the moment, the effect of the shift in perspective was to revive flagging public interest. The restrained formality of the Queen's earlier public persona was replaced by the impression of a homely, relaxed, apparently ordinary individual occupying the role of Queen. As a result, revived attention was accompanied by greater acceptance and even affection.

At the centre of these sentiments was a renewed sense of the Queen's significance in embodying family values. The new image of the Queen at the centre of a model family was an extension of themes advanced in earlier family photographs by Snowdon and Beaton. However, whereas those earlier photographs of royal domesticity retained a certain formality, there was now an impetus towards understatement. Not only was the Queen seen as a more down-

to-earth individual sharing recognisable feelings and needs, but as a mother she represented certain fundamental, nurturing values. At a time when society's morals and principles were tending towards a more liberal outlook, for many the Queen provided a standard of stability and reassurance. These qualities, emphasising apparent ordinariness and the importance of family life, form the basis of the new wave of images of the Queen that circulated from the early 1970s.

Patrick Lichfield's official Silver Wedding photograph encapsulates the gravitation towards a new informality (page 99). Taken at Windsor Castle in December 1971, Lichfield's group portrait achieved a relaxed approachability that seems light years away from the earlier wedding group posed by Alexander Bassano in 1947. Bassano's arrangement presented a stiff, even rigid, pyramidal hierarchy. By contrast, Lichfield produced a much softer, varied composition. The Queen is shown seated, encircled by members of her family. Variously seated and standing, they are joined by the children, some sitting cross-legged at her feet. The interaction of the figures binds them together, lending the group a loose but close unity. The impression of a relaxed, almost amused, gathering represents subtle but tangible advances in terms of the Queen's public image, with the focus now on an individual radiating connectedness.

A more outwardly relaxed individual emerges from the many photographs that Lichfield took of the Queen in 1971. Perhaps the most notable is that depicting her on the deck of the Royal Yacht *Britannia* (page 97). She is shown leaning forward, laughing unselfconsciously after the photographer had been jokingly ducked by members of the crew. Other photographs taken on the same voyage show her at dinner and at work on her red boxes with her private secretary (pages 95 and 98). All these images advanced further into the territory opened up by *Royal Family*.

The press were not slow to absorb and to project the idea of a more down-to-earth, approachable Queen. A photograph from July 1975 depicts a group of smiling coal-miners enjoying a relaxed conversation with their royal visitor, following a visit by the Queen to Silverwood Colliery, Rotherham (page 101). Although more recent events have accustomed eyes to images of the Queen that present a less formal public manner, this press photograph exemplifies the beginning of that process. It brings before a mass audience a new view of the monarch in which gentle humour is also admitted. Previously, studio photographs and even press photographs reporting royal engagements had focused on the dignity of the sitter or the splendour of the occasion. Here the Queen has relinquished her crown for a miner's helmet. This is a visual substitution that speaks volumes about the direction being taken iconographically. Also surprising is the proximity between the Queen and the miners, an encounter that seems not only immediate but devoid of hierarchy.

Such images demonstrate the way that during the 1970s the Queen's image was effectively reinvented. They present a more vital individual, in tune with the times, less remote and, as a result, increasingly popular. These developments were timely, given the impending celebrations that were planned to mark the Silver Jubilee in 1977. Any anxieties about a possible anti-climax were dispelled by the huge wave of popular affection that gathered momentum. Press photographs taken after the Service of Thanksgiving held at St Paul's Cathedral on 6 June 1977 show the Queen meeting the huge crowds of spectators that thronged the surrounding streets (page 104).

However, the price of this enhanced appeal was a growing familiarity. By appearing to draw closer to ordinary life, the revamped image of the Queen was inevitably exposed to wider changes in society's values and attitudes. The late 1970s were marked by a deteriorating situation economically, and, with rising unemployment, among some there was growing resentment of any hint of privileged status. The punk rock scene that emerged in 1976 provided a vocal and visually arresting focus for disaffected youth. Produced to accompany the release of the single 'God Save the Queen', recorded by the Sex Pistols in 1977, Jamie Reid's images of the Queen (page 102) appropriated and deliberately defaced an earlier formal photographic portrait. Harmless in itself, the gesture was nevertheless intentionally iconoclastic, a visual assault on the monarch and everything she represented. At a deeper level, such images carried a further significance. They signalled the beginning of the new attitude to the Queen, and the royal family in general, that emerged in the 1980s. This would be a decade marked by growing royal celebrity, but a corresponding irreverence in response to the way that this popular status was perceived. This paradox would provoke renewed debate about the role of the monarchy and, in the visual arts, unprecedented experimentation with new ways of representing the Queen.

REPRESENTATION

The evolution of the way the Queen has been represented visually in the last sixty years is much more than a document of her life and reign. Images of the sovereign arise from, and are a record of, changing times, attitudes and values. Such portraits of the Queen reflect critical developments in the role and perception of royalty, but they also hold up a mirror to those wider social changes that form the context for the creation and evaluation of royal image-making. As seen above, images of the Queen have constantly negotiated a balance. On one side they reflect an exalted and historic role, one invested with constitutional, ceremonial and symbolic significance. On the other side, they reveal an individual inhabiting that role and maintaining a relationship with society. The Queen is a figure who stands apart from the world but is, at the same time, inseparable from its advances, reversals and vicissitudes. In the last thirty years, the speed and depth of social change have affected the monarchy profoundly, transforming the way that the Queen has been represented and regarded.

The beginning of that transformation dates from the early 1980s and may be identified with the appearance of Lady Diana Spencer. By late 1980, press interest had begun to speculate about a possible romantic link between Diana and Prince Charles. Events moved swiftly, and in February 1981 there was an official announcement of the couple's engagement. Images of the Queen produced around this time demonstrate the radical shift that coincided with the impending royal marriage. Gilbert and George's collage *Coronation Cross* from 1981 (page 112), comprises forty-nine

postcards. These include thirty-six depicting gothic arches and thirteen reproducing Beaton's Coronation photograph arranged in the form of a cross. Made shortly before the thirtieth anniversary of the Queen's Coronation, this image is at once celebratory and ironic. The Queen has a central position, but the cross arrangement has multiple connotations. As well as possessing historic, national significance, it is also connected with crucifixion. Patrick Lichfield's photograph of Queen Elizabeth with Princess Diana on her wedding day could hardly be more different in atmosphere, and the contrast is revealing (page 115). Taken in the Picture Gallery at Buckingham Palace after the marriage ceremony, it depicts Diana centre-stage. For many the centre of gravity in depictions of royalty was in a new place.

Transmitted by television around the world, the wedding of the Prince and Princess of Wales was seen by an estimated audience of around seven hundred and fifty million people. In terms of profile, the royal family had never been so visible. However, two aspects of this visibility were significant departures. The first was the fascinated adulation accorded to Princess Diana. While this echoed the public response to the Queen's own glamorous image at the beginning of her reign, a new generation of journalists and publishers developed an agenda that promoted an interest in Diana's star-like, celebrity status. The second aspect was the shift of attention away from the Queen and towards the activities and personalities of the younger members of the royal family. With Princess Diana as the focus, the preoccupation of the press and public with the image presented by royalty would continue unabated.

The extent of this popular interest also reflected a growing sense of adversity engulfing the monarchy. Partly this emanated from events affecting the Queen directly, and partly it related to worrying developments of national importance. Against this backdrop, the images of the Queen that emerged reflect a sense of duress and growing instability. In June 1981, during the Trooping the Colour ceremony, a man wielding a gun fired several blanks at the Queen on horseback. That same summer civil unrest, ignited by growing unemployment, exploded, with riots in London, Liverpool and Bristol. In May 1982 British forces landed on the Falkland Islands as a response to the earlier Argentinian annexation of the colony. Just a few months later, the press reported that an intruder had been apprehended after entering the Queen's bedroom at Buckingham Palace. This was a sensational breach, not only of security but of the Queen's closely guarded privacy.

In retrospect, this intrusion seems to mark a symbolic watershed, as if entry had been forced into an entire domain that previously had been sacrosanct. Subsequently, press interest in the private lives of royalty widened, with published reports of marital problems and other personal issues relating to Prince Charles and Princess Diana, Princess Margaret, Princess Anne and Prince Andrew. By the mid-1980s, the Queen and the monarchy had become objects of intense media interest. A photograph published in the *Evening Standard* on 4 November 1982 foreshadows the gathering storm (page 117). It shows the Queen followed in procession by Prince Charles and Princess Diana as part of the State Opening of Parliament. The strain of recent developments is palpable in the facial expressions of those depicted. There is also a sense that, under the glare of this growing exposure, the public mask was beginning to slip.

The relationship of the formal public role with the private person had, since *Royal Family*, been an increasingly contested area in the way the Queen was perceived. The nature of that connection now assumed a new, pointed significance. This idea is the central theme of the four large screen-printed portraits of the Queen made by Andy Warhol in 1985 (pages 119–22). Part of a series entitled *Reigning Queens*, these images appropriated an earlier official Silver Jubilee photograph of the Queen by Peter Grugeon. Warhol manipulated that original formal portrait, simplifying detail and repeating the image as a set of colour variations. The effect is to dehumanise the depicted sitter, creating a glamorised – but unreal – representation that hides the individual's identity. Transformed and repeated, the image of the Queen has become a mass-produced mask. The implication is that the fame courted by royalty – or thrust upon it – is a surface veneer: attractive but artificial and without human substance.

As with Richter's earlier images of the Queen, Warhol's extraordinary royal portraits are neither overtly disrespectful nor obviously reverential. Rather, they demonstrate that, while the Queen remained to some extent removed from the upsurge of media interest, presenting members of the royal family as celebrities was a phenomenon to which the Queen was not immune. Representing her in this unnaturally enhanced way was disturbing, not least because such depictions deliberately flirted with the spectre of superficiality. While the image of royalty presented in the press increasingly emphasised status, fame and popularity, the Warhol portraits form an ambiguous parallel presence, being at once commentary and warning.

From the mid-1980s, the public's perception of the royal family underwent a radical change. While Princess Diana continued to attract excited attention, there were increasingly frequent reports in the press relating to the disintegration of her marriage. At the same time, Prince Andrew's

marriage to the Duchess of York also became the subject of gossip and ridicule. In 1987, the idea of involving various younger members of the royal family in a televised game show, *It's a Royal Knockout*, backfired spectacularly. The collective effect of these developments was to undermine the earlier identification of monarchy with family values and to present the royal family not only as dysfunctional but also as figures of fun. From 1984 to its demise in 1996, the satirical television show *Spitting Image* provided a focus for this sea change in public opinion. Once again, an image of the Queen, in this instance a caricatured puppet (above), reflected the wider royal context.

The proliferation of images of royalty in the press in the 1980s can be seen partly as the result of calculated exposure by those depicted, and partly as the response to an increasingly intrusive public.

In the space of a decade, adulation had turned to mockery. During the 1990s, the perception of the institution personified by the Queen became one of bewildered dismay. At the beginning of the decade there were adverse press reports about the Duchess of York's extra-marital relationships, and subsequently she and Prince Andrew announced a separation. Shortly after, in April 1992, Princess Anne and her husband Mark Phillips were divorced. In the same year, after a high-profile unaccompanied tour to India, Princess Diana increasingly projected the persona of a solitary figure. Following Princess Margaret's earlier divorce, these events shattered the image of the Queen as the head of a model family. The year 1992 – the fortieth anniversary of the Queen's accession to the throne – reached a disastrous conclusion with the news that Windsor Castle had been partly destroyed by fire. The photographs of the Queen released in the press were vividly real and strangely symbolic (page 127). Shown accompanied by a fireman, the monarch suddenly appears diminutive and vulnerable. Her face registers bewilderment as the scale of the disaster sinks in. Such images presented a disturbing and unprecedented view of royalty, for they depicted a helpless individual at the centre of an unfolding crisis.

The tragic death of Diana, Princess of Wales following a car crash in 1997 formed the denouement for this all-too-public drama. The institution represented by the Queen had lost its most controversial member, a figure who had attracted and alienated support in equal measure. The display of public feeling that ensued after her death was, however, unambiguous. The unpredictable result of this catastrophe was its effect on the image and perception of the Queen. Yet again, a press photograph provided graphic evidence of deeper currents of change (page 129). Published in *The Times* on 6 September 1997, the Queen and Prince Philip, both wearing black, are shown as if rising from a sea of floral tributes to Diana left by members of the public outside the gates of Buckingham Palace. Among images of the Queen in a public setting, this is one of the most surreal. More strange still, it marks the beginning of a renaissance in the public's perception of the Queen. It intimates a woman sharing in the widespread sense of shock, dignified and commanding respect, now the renewed focus for the nation's collective attention.

The death of Diana, Princess of Wales was an emotive event that inevitably posed questions about the current state and future of the monarchy. At the beginning of the twenty-first century, and with the Queen's Diamond Jubilee in prospect, one question in particular is pertinent: what now does the Queen represent? Artists and other image-makers have responded in various ways. A memorable press photograph taken in July 1999 shows the Queen taking tea with a Scottish family in their Glasgow home (page 133). This understated image advances an accessible Queen, meeting ordinary people in day-to-day situations. Lucian Freud's controversial portrait of 2001 (page 139) presents a not unrelated view, emphasising a fallible human being in an exalted role. Characteristically, Freud's view of his sitter is an unflinching one, executed without the faintest trace of flattery. With her crown balanced somewhat precariously, the Queen is presented as a woman burdened with tradition and the trappings of state, striving stoically to maintain dignity in an age alert to irony. As with Freud's best work, the portrait has an affecting humanity.

Others, such as Hiroshi Sugimoto, present an opposing perspective (page 135). His photograph of the Madame Tussaud's wax model of the Queen is deliberately disorientating. Rather than depicting the real person, a living and feeling individual, it substitutes a somewhat unconvincing mannequin looking like an awkward impostor. Sugimoto presents a view of royalty that appears insulated from the modern world by its own artifice. Cut off from reality, the Queen has become an ambiguous and more abstract presence: pure representation, an image of an image.

More recently, Chris Levine and Annie Leibovitz have, in their respective ways, probed the long-standing question of the relation between the reality of monarchy and its outward appearance. Levine's startling photographic portrait *Lightness of Being* of 2007 (page 149) shows the Queen with her eyes closed. This is an image of supreme inner serenity and equanimity, a personification that is at once immediate and remote. According to the artist, this arresting evocation of royalty came

about unexpectedly during the course of the sitting. Levine's use of long exposures proved tiring for the Queen and there was a brief moment, while she was resting, when the sitter seemed both to relax and to withdraw into herself. Paradoxically, that moment of inner communion conveyed something more palpable and compelling than any of the positions or expressions she had adopted earlier in the session. Levine was able to capture this apparition. The result is one of the most haunting but telling evocations of royalty by any artist. Poised in the void created by suspended self-consciousness, the person inhabiting the role seems illuminated.

Leibovitz's photograph (page 152) is similarly timeless. But where Levine summons a fugitive impression, Leibovitz's portrait casts a line across the years, as if flickering across a surface of different moments from the Queen's reign. Presenting the monarch as a central presence in a natural setting,

Leibovitz draws upon Annigoni's first great portrait of the young Queen. Depicting the Queen wearing a buttoned cape also implies Annigoni's second, less romanticised portrait of the older, more experienced royal incumbent, as well as Beaton's photographic portrait of 1968, with its somewhat secular view of royalty. These earlier images inhabit Leibovitz's frame of reference, but such allusions are refracted through a contemporary sensibility. Like her predecessors, Leibovitz presents the Queen as an enduring, indomitable figure. But seen against a backdrop of turbulent skies, she now appears as a constant within an unpredictable world.

During her reign, images of the Queen have taken innumerable different forms, and perhaps this very fact is in itself revealing about the manifold, elusive nature of the subject. While the occupant and her public role are real and tangible, the monarchy remains an abstraction:

a mutable ideal, open and responsive to change. For over sixty years the Queen has sustained these different elements, negotiating a balance between the individual, her duties and what those duties represent. At the beginning of the twenty-first century, there is a sense that she has become the vital representative of her times, providing a reassuring link with the past and reflecting the present, as those around her confront an uncertain future. In that respect, the Queen eludes any single, definitive visual representation, but inspires a paradox best captured by the poet T.S. Eliot:

> Time present and time past
> Are both perhaps present in time future
> And time future contained in time past.[15]

[1] See David Cannadine, 'The Context, Performance and Meaning of Ritual: the British Monarchy and the "Invention of Tradition", c.1820–1977' in Eric Hobsbawm and Terence Ranger (eds.), *The Invention of Tradition* (Cambridge: Cambridge University Press, 1983, reprinted 2010), pp.101–64. Cannadine's essay illuminates the extent to which elements of royal tradition were modern innovations.

[2] L. Harris, *Long to Reign Over Us? The Status of the Royal Family in the Sixties* (London: Kimber, 1966), p.75, quoted in Andrew Rosen, *The Transformation of British Life 1950–2000: A Social History* (Manchester: Manchester University Press, 2003), p.39.

[3] Gallup poll in the *Sunday Times*, 14 February 1993, quoted in Rosen, op. cit.

[4] *News Chronicle*, 10 April 1947, quoted in Ben Pimlott, *The Queen: Elizabeth II and the Monarchy* (London: HarperCollins, 1996), p.120.

[5] Quoted in Pimlott, op. cit., p.152.

[6] Ibid., p.180.

[7] Winston Churchill, as reported in *The Times*, 8 February 1952, quoted in Pimlott, op. cit., p.180.

[8] Pimlott, op. cit., p.207.

[9] Winston Churchill, 'Address of Sympathy', House of Commons, 11 February 1952, quoted in Sarah Bradford, *Elizabeth: A Biography of Her Majesty The Queen* (London: Heinemann, 1996), pp.174–5.

[10] Quoted in Bradford, op. cit., p.211.

[11] *New Statesman*, 22 October 1955, quoted in Pimlott, op. cit., p.276.

[12] Cited in S. Clark, *Palace Diary* (London: Harrap, 1958), p.208, quoted in Pimlott, op. cit., p.285.

[13] Quoted in Malcolm Rogers, *Elizabeth II: Portraits of Sixty Years* (London: National Portrait Gallery, 1986), p.85.

[14] Advertisement for *Royal Family*, 1969.

[15] T.S. Eliot, *Four Quartets* (New York: Harcourt Brace, 1943).

1950s

**Queen Elizabeth II arrives
at London Airport**

7 February 1952

Press Association

This photograph provided an expectant
public with its first glimpse of the new
Queen. Having received the news of
her father's death while on tour in
Kenya, Elizabeth immediately returned
to London, where she was greeted by
dignitaries and the press waiting at the
airport. The picture was taken seconds
after she stepped onto the tarmac.

Queen Elizabeth II

Dorothy Wilding, 1952

Chlorobromide print, 290 x 215mm

National Portrait Gallery, London (NPG P870(5))

Dorothy Wilding first photographed
the Queen in 1937 at the Coronation
of her father, King George VI. She
subsequently made portraits of the
Queen on significant occasions. To mark
her accession, Elizabeth posed for the
photographer fifty-nine times, wearing
gowns by Norman Hartnell. Copies
of the best images were sent to every
embassy in the world and appeared on
banknotes and millions of stamps.

Queen Elizabeth II
Dorothy Wilding (hand-coloured
by Beatrice Johnson), 1952
Hand-coloured bromide print, 316 x 248mm
National Portrait Gallery, London (NPG x125105)

Colour applied by hand to Wilding's
photograph produces an image of the
Queen that is at once more naturalistic
than the monochrome original and
also more artificial. Naturalism and
artifice are themes running through the
subsequent iconography of the Queen.

**The Queen broadcasts
to the nation**
December 1952
Camera Press

The Queen's first Christmas message
was broadcast live on the radio from
her study at Sandringham, Norfolk.
This photograph shows her seated at
the same desk that both her father and
grandfather used for their Christmas
broadcasts. She began her message by
paying tribute to her late father.

THE QUEEN ART & IMAGE

The Coronation

2 June 1953

Still from newsreel film footage

British Pathé Ltd

For the first time the coronation of a
British monarch was made visible to
a mass domestic audience via film and
television. The service began with words
from the Archbishop of Canterbury,
'Sir, I here present unto you Queen
Elizabeth, your undoubted Queen.' It
concluded with the acclamation: 'God
save Queen Elizabeth. Long live Queen
Elizabeth. May the Queen live for ever!'

Queen Elizabeth II

Cecil Beaton, 2 June 1953

Semi-matt cibachrome print, 331 x 249mm

National Portrait Gallery, London (NPG x35390)

Beaton's Coronation photograph
was taken in the Picture Gallery at
Buckingham Palace after the ceremony.
His impression was of an individual
'cool, smiling, sovereign of the situation'.
Watching on television, an estimated
twenty-seven million people had seen
the Archbishop of Canterbury place
St Edward's crown on Elizabeth's head.
Beaton's photograph shows her wearing
the Imperial State crown, in which are
set the Black Prince's ruby and Queen
Elizabeth I's pearl earrings.

**The Queen leaving
the London Palladium**
Monty Fresco, 1954
Camera Press

During the early years of her reign the
Queen continued to make occasional
anonymous informal outings when it
was still possible to pass unobserved.
Such excursions became curtailed as
television and published photographs
made her instantly recognisable. As
this photograph of the Queen leaving
the Royal Variety Performance shows,
exposure in the media emphasised her
qualities of elegance and glamour.

Queen Elizabeth II

Cecil Beaton, 1955

Bromide print, 429 x 355mm

National Portrait Gallery, London (NPG x26017)

Here the Queen is portrayed as
Sovereign of the Most Noble Order
of the Garter. As in his Coronation
photograph, Beaton employs a
photographic backdrop, in this case
based on a watercolour of Windsor
Castle, where the annual St George's
Day procession and service of the Order
are held. The effect of this device is
to emphasise not only the formality
of the image, but also its artifice.

**Queen Elizabeth II
and Cecil Beaton**

Unknown photographer, 1955

Modern print from 10 x 8-inch colour
transparency, 380 x 480mm

National Portrait Gallery, London
(NPG x40655)

Beaton portrayed the royal family
on numerous occasions, the Queen
and Queen Mother being frequent
sitters. Beaton did not seek to impress
with bravura technical effects but
relied instead on carefully creating a
compelling relationship between the
sitter and the setting. This photograph
captures Beaton at work, arranging
the Queen's pose for the image he
is creating.

Queen Elizabeth II, Queen Regent

Pietro Annigoni, 1954–5

Oil on canvas, 1633 x 1133mm

The Fishmongers' Company

Regarded as one of the greatest royal portraits of the twentieth century, Annigoni's painting was prompted by an observation made by the Queen while the artist was making a preparatory sketch: 'When I was a little child, it always delighted me to look out of the window and see the people and traffic going by.' The compelling image that resulted suggests an individual gazing at the world from a position of isolation.

**Princess Anne, Prince Charles,
Queen Elizabeth II and
Prince Philip**
Antony Armstrong-Jones,
10 October 1957
Bromide print, 286 x 230mm
National Portrait Gallery, London
(NPG x32733)

Alongside formal studio images of
the Queen by Wilding and Beaton,
photographs such as this one by Antony
Armstrong-Jones (later Lord Snowdon)
presented the Queen with her family
and emphasised domestic themes. Such
images conveyed a sense that, beneath
the mantle of her unique position, the
Queen shared everyday human values.

**The Queen makes her first
televised Christmas broadcast**
25 December 1957
Press Association

In 1957 the Queen made the first
televised Christmas Day address.
Broadcast live, this significant event
brought the Queen into the living rooms
of the nation, cementing the public
perception of the monarch as
the embodiment of family values.

1960s

Queen Elizabeth II with the infant Prince Andrew and Prince Edward

Cecil Beaton, 1964

Bromide print, 281 x 216mm

National Portrait Gallery, London

(NPG x26038)

Queen Elizabeth II with the infant Prince Andrew

Cecil Beaton, 1960

Bromide print, 493 x 295mm

National Portrait Gallery, London

The Queen gave birth to her third child and second son, Prince Andrew, on 19 February 1960. Beaton's intimate photograph of mother and infant was taken the following month (right). This, and his later photograph of the Queen with Princes Andrew and Edward, taken in 1964 (left), departed from the formality of his earlier royal portraits. Drawing closer, they focus instead on the Queen's role as a protective parent.

**The Queen addresses
her largest-ever audience**
Delhi, 28 January 1961
Press Association

During the six-week tour of the Indian
subcontinent in early 1961, the Queen
was welcomed by half a million people
in the streets of Delhi. Avoiding the
implication of lingering authority,
the republics of India and Pakistan
greeted their visitor as Queen of the
United Kingdom rather than Head of
the Commonwealth. Even so, as this
image suggests, the Queen continued
to exercise a compelling hold on the
attention and imagination of vast
audiences.

Queen Elizabeth II
Yousuf Karsh, 1966
Cibachrome print, 343 x 263mm
National Portrait Gallery, London (NPG P339)

A Canadian photographer of Armenian
extraction, Yousuf Karsh photographed
the Queen on four occasions over a
period of forty years. This photograph,
which belongs to the third session,
in 1966, emphasises the sitter's regal
splendour. The Queen is shown wearing
the Russian fringe tiara (a gift to Princess
Alexandra in 1888) and the Garter
Sash and Star. Pinned to the sash are
Royal Family Orders of George V and
George VI.

Elizabeth I

Gerhard Richter, 1966

Lithograph on paper, 700 x 595mm

Tate

In May 1965 the Queen visited Germany, the first British sovereign to do so in over fifty years. In Berlin she was cheered and her name chanted. The following year the German artist Gerhard Richter made two lithographs of the Queen, entitled *Elizabeth I* and *Elizabeth II*. In common with much of his work at that time, the prints were based on a published photograph. The original image is blurred, emphasising a sense of surface appearance obscuring the underlying reality.

Queen Elizabeth II

Gerhard Richter, 1967

Oil on canvas, 620 x 530mm

Museum Wiesbaden

Following his earlier lithographs of the Queen, in 1967 Richter made this painted portrait. Like the previous image, it was based on a published photograph. In contrast to the print, Richter has exaggerated his subject's features, removing subtle detail and emphasising colour. In common with the blurred portrait, the effect is to produce an abstracted image, heightening the impression of artifice.

Queen Elizabeth II
Cecil Beaton, 16 October 1968
Cibachrome print from original
transparency, 333 x 332mm
National Portrait Gallery, London
(NPG x29298)

Taken for the exhibition of Beaton's
work held at the National Portrait
Gallery in 1968–9, this understated
image demonstrates the photographer's
gravitation towards more informal
portraits of the Queen. Although the
pose retains a suggestion of formality,
the monarch is shown wearing an
admiral's boat cloak, a device that
echoes Annigoni's celebrated portrait
of 1954–5. Indeed, Beaton referred
to this photograph as 'the poor man's
Annigoni'.

**The Queen presents the
Jules Rimet Cup to Bobby Moore
at the World Cup Final**
30 July 1966
Getty Images

The Queen is shown here at one of
the defining moments in Britain in the
1960s, presenting the Jules Rimet Cup
to Bobby Moore, captain of the England
football team, on the occasion of their
victory over West Germany in the World
Cup Final.

Queen Elizabeth II

Eve Arnold, 1968

Cibachrome print, 432 x 295mm

National Portrait Gallery, London

(NPG P520)

The American photojournalist Eve
Arnold joined Magnum Photos in
1951. After moving to Britain in the
early 1960s, she worked for the *Sunday
Times* and began to use colour as part of
her practice. In contrast to conventional
portraits that emphasised the Queen's
special – but remote – position, Arnold's
startlingly spontaneous photograph
emphasises the Queen's qualities as
an apparently ordinary, approachable
person.

Royal Family

Joan Williams, 1968

Production still

Camera Press

Broadcast twice in June 1969, Richard
Cawston's filmed television documentary
Royal Family was seen by almost 70
per cent of the British population and
radically changed the public perception
of royalty. For the first time, cameras
were admitted behind the scenes, and
the Queen was seen speaking informally
in private situations. The image that
emerged revealed the Queen as an
individual, greatly influencing the way
she would be represented in the future.

Queen Elizabeth II
Pietro Annigoni, 1969
Oil on panel, 1981 x 1778mm
National Portrait Gallery, London
(NPG 4706)

Commissioned by the National Portrait Gallery, Annigoni's second portrait of the Queen was unveiled in 1970 to enormous public and press interest. Reaction focused on the contrast with Annigoni's earlier portrait, which presented a romantic, idealised view. The new portrait adopted a radically different approach. The artist explained: 'I did not want to paint her as a film star; I saw her as a monarch, alone in the problems of her responsibility.'

1970s

**Queen Elizabeth II with Jomo
Kenyatta and Mama Ngina**

Patrick Lichfield, 1970s

Cibachrome print, 207 x 291mm

National Portrait Gallery, London

(NPG x29566)

The Queen is seen here with Jomo
Kenyatta, the first Premier and President
of the Republic of Kenya, and his wife.
As overseas representative, the Queen
was actively involved in making foreign
visits and receiving visitors, but during
the early 1970s this role brought her
into conflict with Edward Heath, her
Prime Minister at that time. Heath
was a passionate European who took
a different view about maintaining
relations with the Commonwealth and
with African states.

**Queen Elizabeth II
with Martin Charteris**

Patrick Lichfield, 1971

Cibachrome print, 206 x 291mm

National Portrait Gallery, London

(NPG x29568)

Every day since her accession the Queen
has dealt with her 'boxes' – leather-
covered cases containing documents for
her attention and signature. Lichfield's
photograph shows her with Martin
Charteris, her Private Secretary at that
time, on board the Royal Yacht *Britannia*
in 1971.

Queen Elizabeth II
Patrick Lichfield, 1971
Cibachrome print, 610 x 477mm
National Portrait Gallery, London
(NPG x29562)

Among informal images of the Queen, Lichfield's photograph ranks as one of the most spontaneous. It shows her on board the Royal Yacht *Britannia* after it had crossed the equator. Lichfield, having been ducked by the crew to mark this passage, used a waterproof camera to capture the Queen's amused reaction. Launched in 1953, *Britannia* was in royal service for forty-four years.

Queen Elizabeth II
Patrick Lichfield, 1971
Cibachrome print, 386 x 258mm
National Portrait Gallery, London
(NPG x29567)

Taken in spring 1971, Lichfield's
informal images of the Queen on
board the Royal Yacht *Britannia* include
this captivating glimpse of a relaxed
monarch at dinner.

**Official group photograph to mark
the Silver Wedding anniversary
of Queen Elizabeth II and
Prince Philip**
Patrick Lichfield, 26 December 1971
Colour print, 382 x 495mm
National Portrait Gallery, London
(NPG x26200)

This group portrait was taken at
Windsor Castle to mark the Queen
and the Duke of Edinburgh's Silver
Wedding anniversary. Lichfield's
arrangement portrays a family gathering
without rigid formality.

**Queen Elizabeth II
visiting Princess Anne**

C. Travis, 8 July 1971

Sunday Times/NI Syndication

The Queen was confronted by
photographers when she visited Princess
Anne at King Edward VII's Hospital,
London, in July 1971, where she had
been undergoing an operation. The
growth of interest in the private lives
of members of the royal family was
sustained by an increasingly intrusive
press, whose attention was no longer
confined to state occasions.

**The Queen on a visit to
Silverwood Colliery, Rotherham**
30 July 1975
Press Association

This press photograph is remarkable not
only for the unusual headwear adopted
by the coal-miners' royal visitor, but also
for the direct, close contact between
the Queen and the men. Such images
effectively reshaped public perception
of the monarch by representing
her in a more down-to-earth light,
communicating with ordinary people
on the same level.

God Save the Queen

Jamie Reid, 1977

Promotional poster, 700 x 990mm

Victoria and Albert Museum

Shortly before the Queen's Silver Jubilee, on 22 May 1977, the punk rock band the Sex Pistols released their second single, 'God Save the Queen'. The song's controversial lyrics linked the Queen with 'a fascist regime' and it was banned by the BBC. The image devised by Jamie Reid for the record cover and related publicity was similarly provocative; a visual assault in a society less inclined to deference.

**The Queen after the Service of
Thanksgiving for the Silver Jubilee**

7 June 1977

Press Association

The Queen's Silver Jubilee was a
huge popular success. On 7 June 1977
a million people lined The Mall to
watch the State Coach take the Queen
and Prince Philip to the Service of
Thanksgiving at St Paul's Cathedral.
While the numbers equalled those for
the Coronation, the Jubilee images
reflect an entirely different relationship
between the public and an increasingly
accessible monarch.

**Queen Elizabeth II
and Peter Phillips**

Snowdon, 1978

Bromide print, 325 x 329mm

National Portrait Gallery, London

(NPG x29572)

As this photograph by Snowdon
demonstrates, the importance of family
values remained a key element in the
image presented by the Queen. Here
she is shown holding her first grandchild,
Peter Phillips, who was born on
16 November 1977.

1980s

Queen Elizabeth II, Queen Elizabeth, the Queen Mother and Princess Margaret

Norman Parkinson, 1980

Cibachrome print, 394 x 495mm

National Portrait Gallery, London

(NPG P200)

Taken to mark Queen Elizabeth, the Queen Mother's eightieth birthday in August 1980, this photograph by Norman Parkinson emphasises stability and the close bonds of family. Within a short period of time the royal family would experience enormous internal and external pressures, and its members would be both celebrated and vilified in the press.

Elizabeth and Philip Potent

Gilbert and George, 1981

Postcards and paper collage on paper,

1330 x 997mm

From the Private Collection

of Mr and Mrs Ellis

Gilbert and George's postcard collage
brings together images of the Queen
and Prince Philip within an heraldic
arrangement known as a cross potent
or crutch cross. The symbolism is
deliberately ambiguous. While the image
seems overtly patriotic, the cross potent
symbol was used by the Vaterländische
Front, the Austrian Fascist Party, in the
1930s. The reference to 'potent' carries
multiple connotations; a 'cross potent'
is a traditional heraldic symbol, but also
implies both power and male sexuality.

ELIZABETH AND PHILIP POTENT

Gilbert and George   1981

CORONATION CROSS

Coronation Cross

Gilbert and George, 1981

Paper collage on board, 1330 x 997mm

Tate

Like *Elizabeth and Philip Potent*, this related postcard arrangement by Gilbert and George can be viewed in different ways. Incorporating copies of Cecil Beaton's Coronation photograph, the collage refers to earlier royal splendour. But the arrangement of these images in a cross shape can be seen as carrying nationalistic connotations, as well as alluding to crucifixion.

Queen Elizabeth II with
Princess Diana on her wedding day

Patrick Lichfield, 29 July 1981

Cibachrome print, 250 x 385mm

National Portrait Gallery, London (NPG x29570)

Taken shortly after the wedding of the
Prince and Princess of Wales, Patrick
Lichfield's photograph of the Queen,
Princess Diana and her bridesmaids
encapsulates the dynamics of a situation
that would come to dominate the image
of royalty in the 1980s. Diana is centre-
stage, radiant. The Queen stands
somewhat apart, dignified but removed,
as a younger generation forms the focus
of attention.

**The Queen performs the State
Opening of Parliament with the
Prince and Princess of Wales**
3 November 1982

Evening Standard

In late 1982 the press noted the
pressures imposed on the Queen by
a sequence of earlier events. British
troops were sent to war to recover the
Falkland Islands, an intruder broke into
her bedroom, terrorist attacks resulted
in the death of soldiers belonging to the
Household Cavalry, and the Queen's
private detective resigned, accused of
involvement with a male prostitute.
Unusually, in this photograph such
strains are evident in the Queen's
expression.

Queen Elizabeth II
Andy Warhol, 1985
Silkscreen prints, 1000 x 800mm each
National Portrait Gallery, London
(NPG 5882(1–4))

Andy Warhol was fascinated by fame.
From the early 1960s his images of
celebrities dissected the relationship
between the individual and his or her
public persona. It is significant that
in 1985 he turned to the Queen as a
subject ripe for this treatment. Based
on a photograph by Peter Grugeon,
the resulting screen-printed images
transformed the Queen's features
through abstraction and exaggerated
colour. The implication is that the public
face is pure artifice.

1990s

The Queen with a fireman
at Windsor Castle

Dylan Martinez, 21 November 1992

Reuters

In late 1992 a picture restorer's lamp set fire to curtains at Windsor Castle. The resulting blaze devastated parts of the castle, including the State Dining Room. The Queen rushed to the scene, and her shocked response was captured by press photographers. Coming at the end of a year that saw several damaging news stories about the royal family, this image seems to symbolise what the Queen later called her *annus horribilis*.

**The Queen and Prince Philip
survey floral tributes after the
death of Diana, Princess of Wales**

Peter Nicholls, 5 September 1997

The Times/NI Syndication

The death of Diana, Princess of Wales
as the result of a high-speed car crash
in Paris on 31 August 1997 caused
worldwide shock. In London floral
tributes were piled outside the gates
at Buckingham Palace and at other
locations. The Queen was criticised
for failing to make a public statement.
On 5 September she was photographed
surveying a sea of flowers and later
made a live broadcast. Both actions
helped to restore public confidence
in her.

The Queen meets the Spice Girls

Richard Pohle, 1 December 1997

The Times/NI Syndication

Following the death of Diana, Princess
of Wales, the image presented by the
Queen underwent a change of style.
There was a new impetus to modernise,
to appeal to a younger generation, and
to be seen to participate more closely in
wider social trends. Here the Queen is
shown meeting the pop group the Spice
Girls, then at the height of their success.

THE QUEEN ART & IMAGE

The Queen

Justin Mortimer, 1998

Oil on canvas, 1350 x 1350mm

RSA

Commissioned by the Royal Society
for the Encouragement of Arts,
Manufactures and Commerce, Justin
Mortimer's portrait of the Queen
was based on drawings made from life
and photographs. The public response
to the artist's use of flattened, cut-out
shapes that seemed to separate the
monarch's head from her body was
adverse. However, at a time when the
Queen was actively seeking a more
modern image, Mortimer's portrait
seemed to strike a chord. The Queen
later commissioned the artist to paint
her Lord Chamberlain.

**The Queen has a cup of tea
with Susan McCarron and her
son, James, in their home in
Castlemilk, Glasgow**
Dave Cheskin, 7 July 1999

Press Association

In the late 1990s, as part of the
imperative to update her image,
the Queen embarked on a series
of visits, meeting ordinary people
informally. Here she is shown with
housing manager Liz McGinnis
(standing) meeting Susan McCarron (left)
and her son, James (back right), in their
home on a Glasgow council estate.

Queen Elizabeth II

Hiroshi Sugimoto, 1999

Gelatin silver print laid on aluminium,

1492 x 1194mm

National Portrait Gallery, London

(NPG P1002)

The Japanese artist Hiroshi Sugimoto
studied photography in Los Angeles.
This strangely disconcerting image of
the Queen, at once lifelike and artificial,
actually shows a wax mannequin. It
forms part of a series of photographs
of wax effigies and tableaux in public
attractions such as Madame Tussaud's
in London. Sugimoto's 'portrait' of the
Queen is an abstraction, an image of
something that is itself unreal.

2000s

Queen Elizabeth II
Lucian Freud, 2001
Oil on canvas, 220 x 150mm
The Royal Collection

Lucian Freud's controversial portrait
was the product of sittings that took
place at St James's Palace between May
2000 and September 2001. Freud was
asked to depict the Queen wearing
the diamond diadem crown that she
wore when photographed by Dorothy
Wilding almost fifty years earlier. The
two images seem to occupy different
worlds. Whereas Wilding responded to
the Queen's youth and glamour, Freud
produced an image emphasising age and
experience.

**The Queen meets a Pearly King
and Queen, east London**

9 May 2002

Press Association

The process of creating a more informal
royal image for the twenty-first century
raised questions about what the Queen
is, her role, and what it means to be a
monarch in a more egalitarian society.
This photograph of the Queen's street
encounter with a Pearly King and
Queen in Newham, east London, reveals
an interesting insight on the back of the
Pearly King's jacket: 'One never knows'.

**The Queen greets the crowds
during her eightieth-birthday
celebrations**

21 April 2006

Press Association

In 2006 the Queen celebrated her
eightieth birthday. Since the 1970s,
attention had shifted from her formal
role, focusing increasingly on the Queen
as an individual. During the 1980s and
1990s public and press interest in the
private lives of members of the royal
family intensified. However, as this
photograph suggests, the Queen has
negotiated changes in the way royalty is
perceived, and public affection remains
strong.

Equanimity

Chris Levine, 2007

Lenticular print on lightbox, 750 x 450mm

Courtesy of the artist

As with *Lightness of Being* (page 149), this image was the result of a commission by the Island of Jersey in 2004 for a portrait of the Queen to commemorate the island's 800-year allegiance to the Crown. Two sittings took place and, to create a three-dimensional portrait, over 10,000 images were made. *Equanimity* was the first holographic portrait of the Queen, producing a virtual effect that cannot be replicated on paper.

The Queen shelters from the rain at the opening of the Lawn Tennis Association's new headquarters in Roehampton
Cathal McNaughton, 29 March 2007

Press Association

In 1969, Annigoni expressed his aim as being to portray the 'monarch, alone in the problems of her responsibility'. Almost fifty years later, this surprising press image aptly conveys the solitude that continues to define the position of the Queen.

Elizabeth vs Diana

Kim Dong-Yoo, 2007

Oil on canvas, 2273 x 1818mm

Courtesy of the artist and

I-MYU Projects, London

This composite image by Korean
artist Kim Dong-Yoo comprises
1,106 individual images of Princess
Diana which, when viewed collectively,
form a portrait of the Queen. Created
just over a decade after Diana's death,
the portrait has a compelling ambiguity,
arising from a sustained tension between
the two elements.

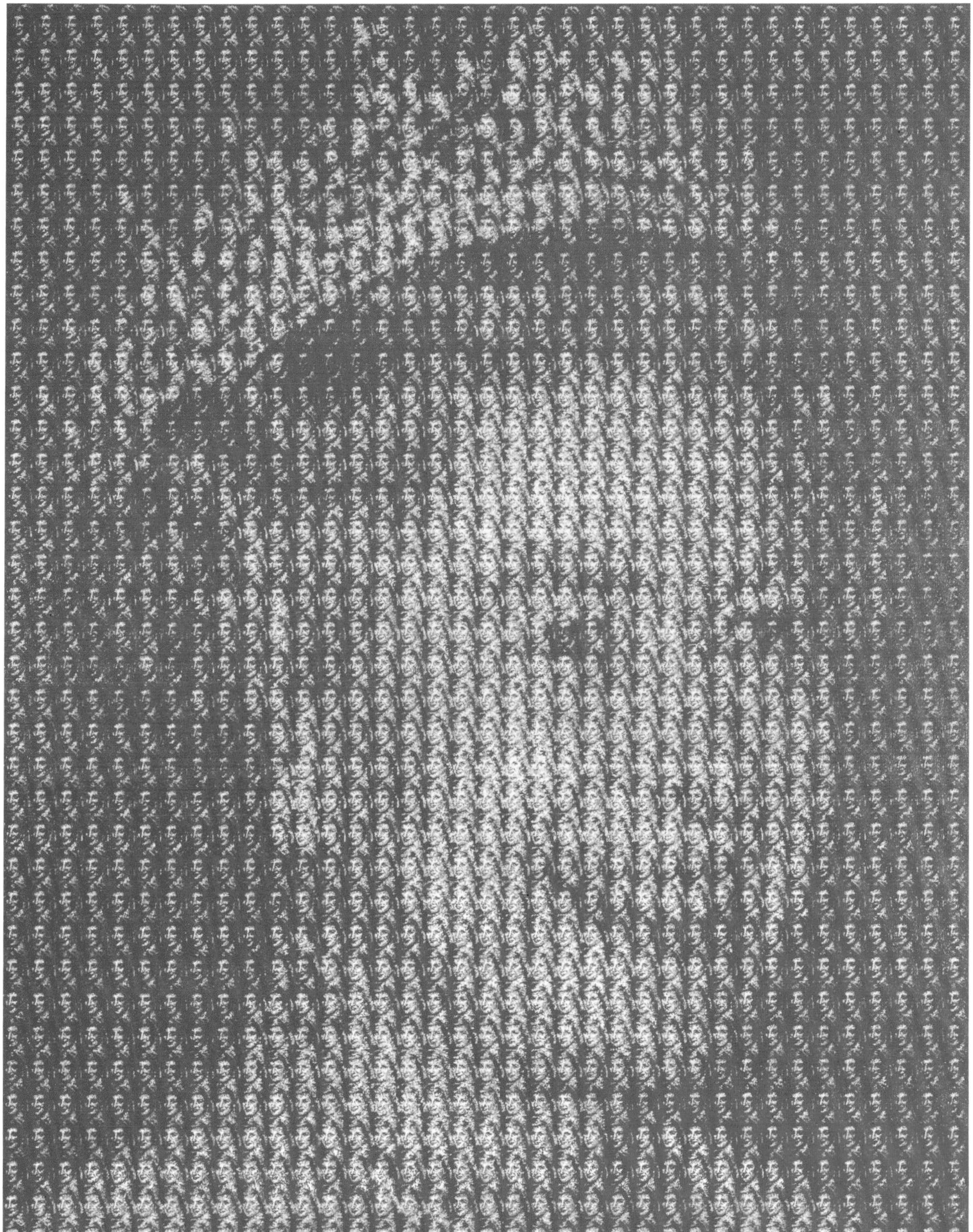

Lightness of Being

Chris Levine, 2007

Print on lightbox, 1400 x 900mm

Courtesy of Mr Kevin P. Burke and
the Burke Children Private Collection

In 2004, as part of Jersey's celebration
of its 800-year relationship with
the monarchy, Chris Levine was
commissioned to make a portrait of the
Queen (page 143). During the sittings
that ensued, each lengthy photographic
exposure took eight seconds. Resting
between shots, the Queen briefly closed
her eyes, a moment preserved by this
image. The resulting portrait seems
poised between the public persona and
the private individual, extremes explored
by artists throughout the Queen's reign.

Medusa

Hew Locke, 2008

Metal, plastic and textile on plywood
and MDF, 2105 x 802 x 204mm

Arts Council Collection, Southbank
Centre, London

This unconventional portrait is part of
a series of mixed-media images of the
Queen created by Hew Locke. Born in
Edinburgh, Locke grew up in British
Guyana, where, during his childhood,
the Queen's image could be found on
the covers of school exercise books.
Returning to that image as an adult,
Locke used cheap, brightly coloured
plastic materials to evoke a likeness that
is at once traditional and subversive.

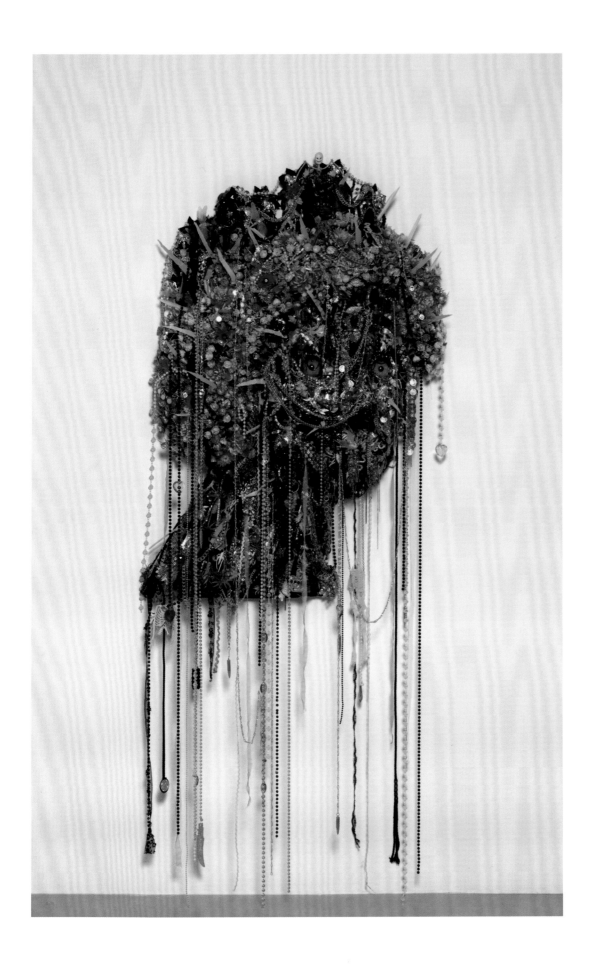

Queen Elizabeth II

Annie Leibovitz, 2007

Chromogenic print, 864 x 1244mm

National Portrait Gallery, London

(NPG P1316)

In 2007 the American photographer
Annie Leibovitz created four magisterial
photographic portraits of the Queen,
of which this is one. Here Leibovitz
returned to themes explored by
Annigoni in 1954–5 and Beaton in
1968. As in those earlier images,
the Queen is depicted as a cloaked,
solitary presence – Leibovitz even
replicating the admiral's cloak used
by Beaton. The result is a striking
contemporary image that draws deeply
on tradition.

CHRONOLOGY

1950s

Queen Elizabeth II, Queen Mary and Queen Elizabeth, the Queen Mother at Westminster Hall during George VI's lying in state, 11 February 1952

1952

On 6 February George VI dies in his sleep at the age of fifty-six after failing to recover from a lung operation. He is succeeded by his eldest daughter, twenty-five-year-old Elizabeth, who learns of his death while on a visit to Kenya. She returns to London the following day. In December, the Queen transmits her first Christmas message on the radio from Sandringham.

1953

The Queen's Coronation on 2 June is the first to be televised. The BBC broadcasts the event live to millions across the nation. Cecil Beaton creates the official Coronation photograph. In November the Queen and Prince Philip embark on a five-and-a-half-month tour of the Commonwealth. The Queen broadcasts her Christmas message by live radio relay from New Zealand.

1954

The Queen and Prince Philip return to London in May, having travelled over 40,000 miles. From October to Christmas there are fifteen sittings for her portrait by Pietro Annigoni, which would come to be celebrated as one of the greatest royal portraits of the twentieth century.

The Queen and Prince
Philip during the royal tour
of Canada, 6 July 1959

Winston Churchill leaving
Downing Street after his
formal resignation from
office, 1 April 1955

1955

Following a period of ill
health, Prime Minister
Winston Churchill resigns
from office and is succeeded
by Anthony Eden. On
31 October, after intense
speculation in the press,
the Queen's sister, Princess
Margaret, announces her
intention not to proceed with
marriage to Group Captain
Peter Townsend, a divorcé.

1956

Following the nationalisation
of the Anglo-French-owned
Suez Canal on 26 July,
Britain, with France and
Israel, mounts a disastrous
military campaign against
Egypt and its President,
Colonel Nasser. Subsequently
forced to accept a UN-
arranged ceasefire, Britain
finds its standing as a world
power is damaged.

1957

Following Eden's resignation
on 10 January, Harold
Macmillan becomes prime
minister. On 22 February,
the Queen agrees that her
husband's official title should
be Prince Philip, Duke of
Edinburgh. In October,
the royal couple begin a
state visit to the USA. At
Christmas the Queen makes
the first televised address to
the nation.

1958

The Queen announces
that Prince Charles will be
created Prince of Wales. She
hosts the last presentation of
debutantes at Buckingham
Palace.

1959

In June and July the Queen
and Prince Philip undertake
a six-week tour of Canada.
On their return it is
announced that they are
expecting their third child.

1960s

Prince Philip, First Lady Jacqueline
Kennedy, the Queen and President
John F. Kennedy at Buckingham
Palace,15 June 1961

1960

On 19 February Prince
Andrew is born. In April
the Queen receives the
French President, Charles
de Gaulle, on a three-
day state visit. On 6 May
Princess Margaret marries
the photographer Antony
Armstrong-Jones (created
Lord Snowdon in 1961).

1961

The Queen and Prince
Philip undertake a six-week
tour of India, Pakistan,
Nepal and Iran. In India
the Queen addresses her
largest-ever audience at a
public meeting at the Ramlila
Grounds outside the walls of
Old Delhi. In November she
visits the new Republic of
Ghana, despite concerns over
President Kwame Nkrumah's
dictatorial and anti-Western
stance.

1962

Following a visit by US
President J.F. Kennedy to
Buckingham Palace in June
1961, the Queen invites his
wife, Jacqueline Kennedy,
to lunch. In the same year
the Queen's Gallery at
Buckingham Palace opens to
the public to display artistic
treasures from the Royal
Collection.

1963

In January Britain's
application to join the
European Common Market
is vetoed by President de
Gaulle. The Queen and
Prince Philip embark
on a two-month tour of
Australasia and the Pacific.
In July, during a state visit to
London by King Paul and
Queen Frederika of Greece,
both royal couples attract
catcalls.

1964

On 10 March 1964 the
Queen's fourth child, Prince
Edward, is born. The
Surveyor of the Queen's
Pictures, Sir Anthony Blunt,
secretly admits to MI5
that he has been involved
with Soviet Intelligence. In
October the Queen makes a
nine-day visit to Canada, and
a report in the *Guardian* refers
to 'the unaccustomed sound
of booing'. Harold Wilson
becomes Prime Minister.

The Queen broadcasts her
first Christmas message in
colour, December 1967

The Queen crowns Prince Charles as
Prince of Wales during a ceremony at
Caernarvon Castle in July 1969

1965

In February the Queen visits
Ethiopia and the Sudan.
In May she becomes the
first British monarch to visit
Germany for fifty-two years.
Anthony Wedgwood (Tony)
Benn, Postmaster General,
fails in his bid to have images
of the Queen's head removed
from stamps.

1966

In the Welsh village of
Aberfan 144 people die
when a school and twenty
houses are buried beneath
a vast slippage of colliery
waste. The Queen and
Prince Philip visit the village.
The German artist Gerhard
Richter produces the first
of two unconventional
portraits of the Queen (the
second in 1967).

1967

A plan by protestors to
impersonate the Queen at
an anti-Vietnam War rally
in Trafalgar Square leads to
disputes in the press. The
Queen's televised Christmas
message is transmitted in
colour for the first time.

1968

Recording of the
documentary *Royal Family*
commences. A BBC/ITV
co-production, Richard
Cawston's film of royal life
includes unprecedented
scenes of informal behaviour
and private conversation.

1969

Royal Family is transmitted
for the first time in June. It
is repeated over the next
eighteen months and shown
around the world. In the
United Kingdom it attracts
more than forty million
viewers. The surge of interest
in royalty continues with
the investiture of Prince
Charles as Prince of Wales at
Caernarvon Castle in July.

1970s

The Queen is greeted by Maoris in New Zealand, during a tour of Commonwealth countries in the Pacific, 15 March 1970

1970

In March the Queen begins a seven-week tour of the Commonwealth countries of the Pacific, including Fiji, New Zealand and Australia. The BBC covers the tour and, after the interest generated by *Royal Family*, crowds are large.

1971

Newspaper speculation focuses on the Queen's personal wealth. The tone of royal press coverage becomes less reverential and more critical. A House of Commons select committee defines the Queen's official duties.

1972

The Queen tours southwest Asia. In May she visits her uncle, the Duke of Windsor (formerly King Edward VIII), who is terminally ill – he dies on 28 May. The Queen's Silver Wedding anniversary is celebrated in the press.

1973

Princess Anne marries Captain Mark Phillips. Britain becomes a member of the European Common Market, a development that carries implications for the Queen as Head of the Commonwealth.

1974

A general election in February produces a hung Parliament, and attention focuses on the Queen's power to invite a politician to form a government during political deadlock. However, after Edward Heath resigns, Harold Wilson returns with a minority administration and, after a further general election in October, a small majority.

Children wave flags
during the Silver Jubilee
celebrations in Fulham,
London, 1 January 1977

Prime Minister Margaret
Thatcher and the Queen,
at a reception during the
Commonwealth Conference in
Lusaka, Zambia, 1 August 1979

1975
Ties with the Commonwealth
are emphasised as the Queen
institutes the Order of
Australia and the Queen's
Service Order, New Zealand.

1976
On 16 March Prime Minister
Harold Wilson announces
his retirement. On the same
day, Buckingham Palace
releases news of Princess
Margaret's legal separation
from Lord Snowdon.
A more critical style of
reporting characterises the
tabloid response to the royal
separation.

1977
The Queen's Silver Jubilee
is celebrated throughout
the Commonwealth. She
embarks on a tour of the
United Kingdom, including
Northern Ireland, despite
the IRA threat. She visits
thirty-six counties in three
months. On 15 November
she becomes a grandmother
when Princess Anne gives
birth to a son, Peter. The Sex
Pistols single 'God Save the
Queen' features Elizabeth II
on its cover.

1978
The Canadian Prime
Minister Pierre Trudeau
proposes the transfer of
the Queen's functions to
the Governor General of
Canada, while retaining the
title Queen of Canada. (This
would lead to the Canada
Act, proclaimed by the
Queen in Canada in 1982.)
Strikes paralyse Britain
during the so-called 'Winter
of Discontent'.

1979
The political crisis in the
United Kingdom deepens as
strikes spread. The Queen
visits the Middle East, and
in Saudi Arabia is welcomed
as an 'honorary man'. Prime
Minister James Callaghan
is defeated in the general
election and is succeeded
by Margaret Thatcher.
On 27 August the Queen's
cousin, Lord Mountbatten,
is assassinated by the IRA.

1980s

The Prince of Wales and his bride Lady Diana Spencer during their wedding ceremony at St Paul's Cathedral, 29 July 1981

1981

On 24 February Buckingham Palace announces the engagement of Charles and Diana. In June a seventeen-year-old boy fires blanks at the Queen while she is riding on horseback during Trooping the Colour. On 29 July an international audience of three-quarters of a billion watches the royal wedding. During the summer there are riots in several cities, including London, Liverpool and Belfast, fuelled by social and racial discontent.

1982

The *Sun* newspaper publishes photographs of the Prince and Princess of Wales on holiday. Princess Diana is shown pregnant and wearing a bikini. On 2 April Argentinian forces invade the Falkland Islands and British troops are sent to recover the territory. On 21 June Princess Diana gives birth to a son, Prince William. In July an intruder breaks into the Queen's bedroom at Buckingham Palace.

1983

In February the *Sun* publishes a story linking Prince Andrew with Koo Stark, a former soft-porn film actress. The Queen issues an injunction against the newspaper. The press begins to publish rumours about Princess Diana's health, suggesting that she is suffering from anexoria nervosa.

1984

On 12 October an IRA bomb explodes at the Grand Hotel, Brighton, during a Conservative Party conference. Five people are killed and many others injured. Newspaper reports about the private lives of younger members of the royal family continue. On 15 September Princess Diana gives birth to a second son, Prince Harry.

1980

In August the Queen Mother celebrates her eightieth birthday. In the autumn Lady Diana Spencer is invited to Balmoral. By November there is mounting press speculation about a relationship between Prince Charles and Diana.

The Queen with James Callaghan, Alec Douglas-Home, Margaret Thatcher, Harold Macmillan, Harold Wilson and Edward Heath at 10 Downing Street to celebrate 250 years of its being the official residence of the British prime minister, 1985

The Queen reassures her horse after a man fires several blanks at her during the Trooping the Colour ceremony, 13 June 1981

1985

The Queen is the subject of a series of silkscreen-printed portraits by Andy Warhol. Prince Andrew meets Sarah Ferguson, his future wife.

1986

The *Sunday Times* publishes a report citing policy differences between the Queen and her Prime Minister, Margaret Thatcher. The Queen is said to believe that the government should be more caring to the less privileged in society. In July Prince Andrew and Sarah Ferguson are married.

1987

The press publishes reports that the Prince and Princess of Wales are leading independent lives. In June Prince Edward, the Duke and Duchess of York and Princess Anne appear in *It's a Royal Knockout*, a television game show. Replacing decorum with knockabout humour, the programme is a watershed in the public's perception of royalty.

1988

The Duchess of York gives birth to her first child, Princess Beatrice. The broadsheet press joins the tabloids in criticism of the royal family. The *Sunday Times* cites the public's 'grotesque appetite for all things royal' and admonishes the younger royals for complicity.

1989

In February the *Sunday Telegraph* notes that, although popular, the royal family has never been more subject to criticism than in modern times.

1990s

The Queen is applauded by Vice-President Dan Quayle and House Speaker Thomas Foley before her address to the US Congress in Washington, 16 May 1991

1990

In March the Duchess of York gives birth to her second child, Princess Eugenie. In July the government provokes a new debate about the Queen's wealth when an increase of 50 per cent in the Queen's civil-list income is announced as part of a ten-year agreement. Margaret Thatcher resigns as Prime Minister in November and is succeeded by John Major.

1991

On 10 February the *Sunday Times* criticises the privileged lifestyle of the younger royals, a rebuke that coincides with the preparation of allied forces for war in Iraq. In May the Queen becomes the first British head of state to address a joint meeting of the US Congress in Washington.

1992

The *Sunday Times* serialises *Diana: Her True Story* by Andrew Morton, which includes damaging revelations about royal life. The *Daily Mirror* publishes photographs of a bare-breasted Duchess of York with a friend, John Bryan. This is followed by 'Dianagate', 'Fergiegate' and 'Camillagate': sensational published tape-recordings involving members of the royal family. On 20 November Windsor Castle is partly destroyed by fire. The Queen refers to 1992 as an *annus horribilis*. On 9 December the Prime Minister announces the separation of the Prince and Princess of Wales.

1993

The Queen and the Prince of Wales begin to pay income tax on a voluntary basis. A Gallup poll reports that four out of five respondents think 'too many members of the [royal] family lead an idle, jet-set kind of existence'.

1994

The Queen is not consulted about the Prince of Wales appearing in an ITV documentary in which he admits adultery. In November *Charles: The Private Man, the Public Role*, a book by Jonathan Dimbleby based on the programme, is published.

The Queen and Prince Philip are photographed by Brian Aris in the White Drawing Room at Buckingham Palace as part of their Golden Wedding celebrations, 1997

The Princess of Wales during an interview with Martin Bashir, 20 November 1995

1995

On 20 November the BBC transmits an interview of Princess Diana by Martin Bashir. The programme is made without the Queen's knowledge and contains numerous revelations about Diana's 'enemies'. The Queen writes to the Prince and Princess of Wales advising them to divorce.

1996

The Duke and Duchess of York divorce in April. In August Charles and Diana's fifteen-year marriage also ends in divorce.

1997

Tony Blair becomes Prime Minister. On 31 August the death of Princess Diana in a car accident in Paris provokes widespread grief and tributes. The Queen is criticised for not flying the Union Flag at half-mast at Buckingham Palace, but makes a live television broadcast on 5 September that transforms public opinion. Diana's funeral is watched by an estimated international audience of 2.5 billion.

1998

The Queen's public appearances demonstrate a move to greater informality. During a state visit to Brunei, her speeches refer repeatedly to 'modernisation'.

1999

The Queen opens the National Assembly for Wales in Cardiff and the Scottish Parliament in Edinburgh. In November, in a surge of popularity for the Queen, Australia votes against becoming a republic.

2000s

The Queen sitting for her portrait with Lucian Freud, 2001

2000

The Queen attends official celebrations to mark the new millennium, including the opening of the Millennium Dome at Greenwich and religious services at Southwark and St Paul's cathedrals. In October she visits the Vatican and has her first meeting with the Pope since 1982.

2001

The Queen is visited by President George W. Bush. The Duke of Edinburgh celebrates his eightieth birthday in June. The Queen's portrait is painted by Lucian Freud.

2002

The Queen celebrates her Golden Jubilee, marking fifty years since her accession. She attends international celebrations and events. On 9 February Princess Margaret dies at the age of seventy-one, following a stroke. On 30 March the Queen Mother dies aged 101.

2003

President Putin visits the United Kingdom, the first visit by a Russian leader in 129 years. Prince William turns twenty-one.

2004

French President Jacques Chirac visits the Queen to mark the centenary of the Entente Cordiale.

An image of the
Queen is used in the
Google logo, 2008

Screen showing the Queen
giving a speech at the
opening of St Pancras
Station, 6 November 2007

2005

On 8 April Prince Charles
and Camilla Parker Bowles
are married at Windsor
Guildhall. The Queen does
not attend the wedding
but joins the subsequent
religious blessing.

2006

The Queen celebrates her
eightieth birthday with a
walkabout in Windsor town
centre. She hosts a lunch for
people also celebrating their
eightieth birthday, a party
for two thousand children at
Buckingham Palace and a
family dinner at Kew Palace.

2007

Tony Blair is succeeded as
Prime Minister by Gordon
Brown. On 20 November
the Queen and the Duke
of Edinburgh celebrate
their Diamond Wedding
anniversary.

2008

An image of the Queen is
used as part of the Google
logo. At Google headquarters
she meets the founder and
president of YouTube and is
photographed uploading a
video to the Royal Channel.

2009

The Queen unveils a
memorial statue in honour
of the late Queen Mother
on The Mall, London.
She re-launches the British
Monarchy website at
Buckingham Palace.

2010s

Prince William and
Catherine Middleton
are photographed by
Mario Testino for the
announcement of their
engagement, 2010

2010

The National Portrait Gallery
commissions the German
photographer Thomas Struth
to create a double portrait of
the Queen and the Duke of
Edinburgh.

2011

On 29 April Prince William
marries Catherine Middleton
at Westminster Abbey. In
June the Duke of Edinburgh
celebrates his ninetieth
birthday.

ACKNOWLEDGEMENTS

This catalogue and exhibition mark the Diamond Jubilee of Her Majesty Queen Elizabeth II, who acceded to the throne on 6 February 1952. From the moment of her accession the Queen has been subjected to relentless scrutiny, and the result has been a vast proliferation of images in all media, from formal painted portraits to holograms. This project arose from the National Portrait Gallery's wish to mark this significant milestone and the associated desire to convey a sense of the rich diversity of ways in which the Queen has been depicted during her reign.

From the outset, a paradox was apparent. Despite her extreme exposure, the Queen as an individual remains largely closed to view. Instead, what we have is a succession of virtual representations that have documented her life, her appearance and her involvement with times that have witnessed radical changes. Such images have shaped the way she is perceived. They also form part of a complex social context and, as such, have much to say about the period from which they arose, their visual language reflecting both artistic values and wider attitudes. Images of the Queen made by formal portraitists, photographers, the mass media and contemporary artists are much more than a record of her appearance. They provide vivid evidence of those deeper currents that influenced how the Queen has been represented and regarded. This premiss is the theme of the current exhibition. It explores images of the Queen in terms of their meaning: not only about the sitter, but about the wider world that coloured their creation.

In curating this exhibition I am indebted to the input and support of numerous individuals. First among these is the Director, Sandy Nairne, who entrusted me with this responsibility. I would also like to thank David Cannadine, whose accompanying essay provides a valuable historical perspective. The exhibition will be shown at four venues, Edinburgh, Belfast, Cardiff and London, and I wish to acknowledge the commitment made by directors and senior colleagues at those partner institutions, in particular David Anderson, Pip Diment, James Holloway, Julie Lawson, Kim Mawhinney, Jim McGreevy and Michael Tooby.

In organising the exhibition, I was expertly assisted by Rosie Wilson and Flora Fricker. Perceptive initial picture research was carried out by Katrina Marcou, who joined the project as an intern from the Courtauld Institute. Significant contributions were made by Michael Barrett, Pim Baxter, Claudia Bloch, Stacey Bowles, Nick Budden, Robert Carr-Archer, Naomi Conway, Amanda Cropper, Laura Down, Andrea Easey, Denise Ellitson, Neil Evans, Ian Gardner, Rosemary Harris, Bernard Horrocks, Lord Janvrin, Celia Joicey, Doug King, Justine McLisky, Lucy Macmillan, Ruth Müller-Wirth, Doris Pearce, Jude Simmons, Liz Smith, Thomas Struth, Christopher Tinker, Sarah Tinsley, Helen Whiteoak and Ulrike Wachsmann. Finally, I am grateful to the many generous lenders to the exhibition.

PAUL MOORHOUSE
Curator of Twentieth-Century Portraits,
National Portrait Gallery, London

FURTHER READING

David Cannadine, 'The Context, Performance and Meaning of Ritual: the British Monarchy and the "Invention of Tradition", *c.*1820–1977', pp.101–64 in **Eric Hobsbawm and Terence Ranger** (eds.), *The Invention of Tradition* (Cambridge: Cambridge University Press, 1983)

Andrew Rosen, *The Transformation of British Life 1950–2000: A Social History* (Manchester: Manchester University Press, 2003)

Ben Pimlott, *The Queen: Elizabeth II and the Monarchy* (London: HarperCollins, 1996)

Sarah Bradford, *Elizabeth, A Biography of Her Majesty The Queen* (London: Heinemann, 1996)

Malcolm Rogers, *Elizabeth II: Portraits of Sixty Years* (London: National Portrait Gallery, 1986)

John Arlott, John Snagge and Sir Gerald W. Wollaston, *Elizabeth Crowned Queen: The Pictorial Record of the Coronation* (London: Odhams Press, 1953)

Kenneth O. Morgan, *The People's Peace: British History 1945–1989*, (Oxford: Oxford University Press, 1990)

David Gibbon (ed.), *The Royal Family at Home and Abroad* (New Malden: Colour Library International Limited, 1976)

Dominic Sandbrook, *Never Had It So Good: A History of Britain from Suez to the Beatles* (London: Little, Brown, 2005)

Dominic Sandbrook, *White Heat: A History of Britain in the Swinging Sixties* (London: Little, Brown, 2006)

ADDITIONAL CAPTIONS AND PICTURE CREDITS

ADDITIONAL CAPTIONS

Frontispiece Queen Elizabeth II by
   Dorothy Wilding, 1952 (detail), page 57
Page 5 Queen Elizabeth II by Cecil Beaton,
   2 June 1953 (detail), page 61
Page 7 *Elizabeth I* by Gerhard Richter,
   1966 (detail), page 80
Page 9 *God Save the Queen*, by Jamie Reid,
   1977 (detail), page 102
Page 11 Queen Elizabeth II by Andy Warhol,
   1985 (detail), page 122
Page 13 *Lightness of Being* by Chris Levine, 2007
   (detail), page 149
Page 54 Queen Elizabeth II by Dorothy Wilding
   (hand-coloured by Beatrice Johnson), 1952
   (detail), page 59
Page 74 Queen Elizabeth II by Cecil Beaton,
   16 October 1968 (detail), page 85
Page 92 Queen Elizabeth II by Patrick Lichfield,
   1971 (detail), page 97
Page 106 Queen Elizabeth II by Andy Warhol,
   1985 (detail), page 119
Page 124 Queen Elizabeth II by Hiroshi Sugimoto,
   1999 (detail), page 135
Page 136 *Equanimity* by Chris Levine,
   2007 (detail), page 143

PICTURE CREDITS

The publisher would like to thank the copyright
holders for granting permission to reproduce the
works illustrated in this book. Every effort has been
made to contact the holders of copyright material,
and any omissions will be corrected in future
editions if the publisher is notified in writing.

Essays
Pages 21 (NPG x12984) © National Portrait Gallery,
London; 22 Popperfoto/Getty Images; 24 and 27
Corbis; 28 © Press Association; 32 (NPG x29866)
© V&A Images; 33 Corbis; 38 The Royal Collection
© 2011, Her Majesty Queen Elizabeth II; 42 (NPG
P338) Given by Yousuf Karsh, 1987 © Karsh/
Camera Press; 43 Hulton Archive/Getty Images;
45 (NPG x35389) Photograph by Studio Lisa,
Camera Press, London; 46 Photograph by Joan
Williams, Camera Press, London; 50 ITV/Rex
Features; 52 © Chris Levine.

Plates
Pages 56, 73, 78, 101, 104, 133, 140–1 and 144
© Press Association; 57 and 59 Given by the
photographer's sister, Susan Morton, 1976 ©
William Hustler and Georgina Hustler/National
Portrait Gallery, London; 60 British Pathé Ltd; 61,
64, 76 and 85 © V&A Images/Victoria and Albert
Museum, London; 62 Photograph by Camera
Press, London; 63 Photograph by Monty Fresco,
Camera Press, London; 67 Given by the executors

of the Estate of Eileen Hose, 1991 © V&A Images/
Victoria and Albert Museum, London; 69 Portrait
by Pietro Annigoni, Camera Press, London; 70
© Snowdon/Camera Press; 77 Given by Cecil
Beaton, 1968 © V&A Images/Victoria and Albert
Museum, London; 79 Given by Yousuf Karsh, 1987
© Karsh/Camera Press; 80 © Gerhard Richter,
2011, Photograph © Tate, London 2011; 83 ©
Gerhard Richter, 2011; 84 © AFP/Getty Images;
86 © Eve Arnold/Magnum Photos; 89 Photograph
by Joan Williams, Camera Press, London; 91 Given
by Sir Hugh Leggatt, 1970 © National Portrait
Gallery, London; 94–5, 97–9 and 115 © Lichfield;
100 C. Travis/*Sunday Times*/NI Syndication; 102
© Jamie Reid Courtesy Isis Gallery, Photograph ©
V&A Images/Jamie Reid; 105 Given by Antony
Armstrong-Jones, 1st Earl of Snowdon, 1980
© Snowdon/Camera Press; 109 Given by the
photographer, 1980 © Norman Parkinson Archive;
111 © Gilbert and George; 112 © Gilbert and
George, Photograph © Tate, 2011; 117 *Evening
Standard*; 119–22 © The Andy Warhol Foundation
for the Visual Arts/Artists Rights Society (ARS),
New York/DACS, London 2011; 127 Reuters/
Dylan Martinez; 128 © Richard Pohle for *The Times*,
London; 129 © Peter Nicholls for *The Times*, London;
130 © Justin Mortimer; 135 © Hiroshi Sugimoto;
139 The Royal Collection 2011 © Lucian Freud; 143
and 149 © Chris Levine; 147 © Kim Dong-Yoo; 151
© Hew Locke; 152 Given by Annie Leibovitz, 2008
Official Portrait of HRH Queen Elizabeth II © 2008
Annie Leibovitz, courtesy of the artist.

Chronology
Pages 156, 157 (right), 160, 162, 164 © Press
Association; 157 (left) Time & Life Images/Getty
Images; 158 Popperfoto/Getty Images; 59 (left)
© BBC; 159 (right) © Reserved/The Royal
Collection; 161 (both) Hulton Archive/Getty
Images; 163 (left) © TopFoto; 163 (right) Corbis;
165 (left) AFP/Getty Images; 165 (right)
Photograph by Brian Aris, Camera Press, London;
166 (NPG x128062) Given by John Morton Morris,
2006 © David Dawson; 167 (both) Photograph by
Camera Press, London; 168 © Mario Testino.

INDEX